P9-CKN-476

West Hills College Coalinga
Fitch Library
DISCARD
300 Cherry Lane
Coalinga, CA 93210

THE FUTURE OF THE INTERNET

Other Books in the At Issue Series:

THE FUTURE OF THE INTERNET

David Bender, *Publisher*
Bruno Leone, *Executive Editor*
Scott Barbour, *Managing Editor*
Brenda Stalcup, *Series Editor*
Charles P. Cozic, *Book Editor*

West Hills Community College District
Fitch Library
Coalinga Campus
DISCARD
Coalinga CA 93210

An Opposing Viewpoints® Series

Greenhaven Press, Inc.
San Diego, California

No part of this book may be reproduced or used in any form or by any means, electrical, mechanical, or otherwise, including, but not limited to, photocopy, recording, or any information storage and retrieval system, without prior written permission from the publisher.

Library of Congress Cataloging-in-Publication Data

The future of the Internet / Charles P. Cozic, book editor.
        p.   cm. — (At issue)
    Includes bibliographical references (p.   ) and index.
    ISBN 1-56510-659-8 (lib. : alk. paper). — ISBN 1-56510-658-X
(pbk. : alk. paper)
    1. Internet (Computer network) I. Cozic, Charles P., 1957–   .
II. Series: At issue (San Diego, Calif.)
ZA4201.F87   1997
004.67'8—dc21   97-22
                                                                  CIP

© 1997 by Greenhaven Press, Inc., PO Box 289009,
San Diego, CA 92198-9009

Printed in the U.S.A.

Every effort has been made to trace owners of copyrighted material.

Table of Contents

Introduction

In 1969, the U.S. Department of Defense's Advanced Research Projects Agency (ARPA) inaugurated ARPANET, a small network of high-speed super-computers designed to withstand military attack. The purpose of ARPANET was to enable researchers and scientists to share one another's computer facilities by long distance for national research and development projects. However, writes author Bruce Sterling, "The main traffic on ARPANET was not long-distance computing. Instead, it was news and personal messages."

Throughout the 1970s and 1980s, ARPANET grew, accommodating many different types of computers, until it was incorporated in 1989 within the National Science Foundation's own computer network, which became known as the Internet. According to Sterling, "Its users scarcely noticed, for ARPANET's functions not only continued but steadily improved." As the availability of personal computers increased, the Internet gradually progressed beyond the purview of military and research institutions into schools, libraries, and the business world.

The Internet has since become the world's fastest-growing communications medium, surpassing fax machines and cellular telephones. What was once a network of four computers in December 1969 is now a vast amalgam of more than forty thousand computer networks accommodating more than fifty million users as of the beginning of 1997.

The development perhaps most responsible for the Internet's astonishing growth was the creation and immediate popularity of the World Wide Web (also called the Web or WWW) in 1991. The Web is a collection of commercial, educational, and personal "Web sites" that contain electronic pages of text and graphics. Other popular features of the Internet include e-mail, an electronic system that now delivers more messages and files than the U.S. Postal Service; and MUDs and MOOs (multi-user dungeon and MUD object oriented, respectively), which are domains where users can chat and play games interactively.

Individuals can spend extraordinary amounts of time and money exploring the Internet. Some users "surf the Net" for as many as eighteen hours in one day, resulting in monthly telephone bills that exceed four hundred dollars. Extensive Internet use is often compared to chemical dependency and gambling and, like these disorders, has prompted the creation of self-help groups, such as Interneters Anonymous and Webaholics. The phenomenon of heavy Internet use inspired Tripod, an on-line membership company, to survey its users in June 1996. Responses from fifty members produced no consensus on whether inordinate Internet use is a serious problem. Respondent Doug Padgett confessed, "My ex-wife tells me she divorced me because I spent more time on the computer than on her!" However, another member maintained that "the Internet is definitely addictive, but it makes the real world a better experience."

On-Line Activities

Ranked by percentage of users who say they do each

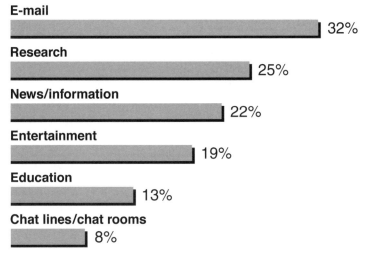

E-mail
32%

Research
25%

News/information
22%

Entertainment
19%

Education
13%

Chat lines/chat rooms
8%

Source: Odyssey Ventures Inc., 1996.

Many observers warn that heavy use of the Internet can have dire, sometimes irreparable, consequences. Lured by the Internet, some users have neglected their relationships and careers, sometimes resulting in ruined marriages and lost jobs. "It's as addictive as alcohol or drugs," according to one forty-three-year-old woman, who told *Newsweek* magazine that her Internet compulsion led to her divorce and estrangement from her children. "I believe it could be really bad and really dangerous for this country," she said.

Students with access to the Internet can also find themselves hooked. Ohio University graduate student Rich Barette states that one reason he started his Webaholics group is that he has two close friends whose academic careers went "down the drain" due to excessive Internet use. In 1996, faculty members at New York's Alfred University found that "nearly half the students who quit [school] had been logging marathon, late-night time on the Internet."

Many mental health professionals and others who had previously doubted whether Internet use could actually be addictive now wholeheartedly believe it is as real an addiction as alcoholism or drug abuse. According to University of Pittsburgh clinical psychologist Kimberly Young:

> I didn't believe it. But I've now heard the same stories from so many people. Use of the Internet can definitely disrupt one's academic, social, financial, and occupational life the same way other well-documented addictions like pathological gambling, eating disorder, and alcoholism can.

Young studied 396 Internet users and presented her findings on what is known as Internet Addiction Disorder (IAD) at the 1996 convention of the American Psychological Association. According to *Cyberia Magazine* writer James Snodgrass, "Internet addicts display the classic symptoms of addictive behavior. They go on-line to escape real-life problems, are unable to control their Internet use, and feel restless and irritable when they try to cut their use."

However, many other experts and computer users deny that IAD is a true disorder or that excessive use of the Internet is much of a crisis. Some observers maintain that most Internet users are nowhere near becoming compulsive users of the medium. *Newsweek* writers Kendall Hamilton and Claudia Kalb point out that "the average TV viewer spends more than 28 hours a week in front of the tube, while the average Interneter burns a comparatively measly five and a half hours." Many users assert that they can easily reduce their Internet time if required. According to a Salem, Massachusetts, computer technician, "I am a cybersurfer down to the marrow, but I could definitely stop if it was doing more damage to my marriage." Other users contend that logging onto the Internet is no more of a problem than spending time on the telephone. As Tripod member "LowKeyCat" notes, "The Internet is a communication tool, just like the telephone, television, and the postal service. I've never heard any of these officially classified as a disorder."

Ardent users contend that exploring the Internet is an extremely enriching experience, a daily ritual that they eagerly look forward to. One benefit of the Internet, proponents maintain, is the development of on-line relationships among users. Tripod member "Quanta" extols the social aspects of the Internet, especially the ability to maintain closer ties with geographically dispersed family and friends:

> In a couple of e-mail discussion groups, strong personal friendships have formed because of the feeling of being connected through various life events experienced by the members of the group. These are the things that create the bonds of community, and this medium has its own unique ways of forming them.

Millions of users are also enthralled by the trove of educational and other useful information available on the World Wide Web with a click of a desktop mouse. Responding to Tripod's survey, a user named "Orbot" wrote, "We don't talk about information addicts when they go for a useless Ph.D. We always understood that the life of the mind is the really important one. How can a society discourage the inquisitiveness of its members?" Fellow member "MarsFire" adds, "There is a wealth of information for me to explore. Let me freely enjoy this."

As in the case of other potentially addictive activities, many observers maintain, whether Internet use becomes detrimental depends on an individual's capacity for self-control. For users who lack adequate self-control, mental health experts recommend setting a daily on-line time limit and sticking to it. They also suggest that users resolve any underlying problems or conflicts that may compel them to spend too much time on the Internet.

As the Internet grows exponentially—"by at least another factor of 100" by the year 2001, according to software developer Charles H. Ferguson— concern toward problematic use of the Internet promises to increase. According to Viktor Brenner, a Marquette University assistant professor of education, "Virtually everything that exists can be found in cyberspace, so the range of persons who use—and might abuse—computers and the Internet is wider than ever before." Nevertheless, Brenner concedes that "we have no data on what types of behaviors would constitute this 'addiction,' its prevalence, or who 'gets addicted.'" Internet addiction is among the issues explored in *The Future of the Internet*, in which authors discuss the phenomenon of the Internet and its impending effects on individuals and society.

1

The Future of the Internet: An Overview

Joe Flower

Joe Flower is principal of The Change Project, a Larkspur, California, consulting organization that specializes in health care and high technology. Flower's articles frequently appear on The Well, a San Francisco–based computer network.

The Internet's popularity has increased tremendously; more than ninety nations now have a direct connection to this network. World Wide Web use accounts for approximately one-half of Internet traffic. The future of the Internet is uncertain, but any of several possibilities could occur: The Internet could become an unrestrained entity, molded according to the diversity of its users; or it could transform into a commercial network dominated by large companies. The network could be threatened if governments decide to monitor Internet communications and transactions. Because it allows a free flow of information, some governments may place restrictions on Internet access.

The Internet had a transplant in April 1995, but the operation didn't seem to bother it one bit. In a process that was completed on 1 May 1995, the US National Science Foundation handed over its responsibility for the Internet's "backbone" to private companies.

For many, the fact that the Internet has a backbone at all will come as a surprise. And the role of the NSF, an agency of the US government charged with serving the needs of researchers, is also often forgotten. Most users of the Internet merely think of the network as a relatively reliable, cheap and bureaucracy-free means of moving information around the world.

So far, so good. Times are changing fast, however. From its relative obscurity as a tool for everyday researchers, the Internet has become a global superstar with the bright but unpredictable future that goes with that status. Now the latest sport from Beijing to Baltimore is to ask some everyday questions. For example, who owns the Internet? Who runs it? Who

Joe Flower, "Idiot's Guide to the Internet," *New Scientist*, July 1, 1995. Reprinted by permission of IPC Specialist Group, London.

10

picks up the tab for transferring and storing all that information? How will fame change it?

Looking for the owner of the Net is a fruitless task—there is no simple answer. Even when its backbone was owned and run by the NSF, the Internet could never be said to have a single owner. The reason for this becomes clear if you look at the network's origins.

Growth of the Internet

It incubated within the so-called military-industrial complex. Together, the employees of military-industrial research laboratories created a network that was like a piece of lace with nodes and connections woven in all over the place. This had various advantages over more traditional network designs, where a central computer was connected to other computers rather like spokes connecting to the centre of a wheel. The lack of a hub meant that there was nothing to be "taken out" in the event of a nuclear strike. It also allowed all sorts of different computers to talk to each other.

Back in the early 1970s, this net was called ARPANET, because it was run by the US Department of Defense's Advanced Research Projects Administration. It linked four supercomputers at key universities and research sites linked by dedicated telephone cables and powerful computer switches to form a high-speed network. This backbone was administered by the NSF from 1988.

Other networks, both in the US and other countries, could link into this network. As the Internet backbone accepted noncommercial traffic from anywhere, so many of the networks that sprung up in university communities and research centres around the world found it quicker to route their traffic through the superfast backbone in the US than to talk directly to each other.

At first, it was mainly American networks that linked into the Internet. But in the past few years the popularity of the Internet outside the US has increased rapidly. By February 1995, over 90 nations had a direct connection to the "core" Internet, the web of machines connected by the TCP/IP protocol—the ground rules of the Internet. This core had links to other worldwide networks—both commercial and educational, such as BITNET, FidoNet, AppleLink, Minitel and UUCP, and reached into 168 countries.

Even at the hardware level—the wires, fibres and routeing equipment—the Internet has no single owner.

The manner in which the Internet has grown has left no one organisation in charge of the network. This network is informally "kludged together". But according to Hal Varian, a professor at the University of Michigan who specialises in the economics of the Internet, "they still have to work the bugs out".

So even at the hardware level—the wires, fibres and routeing equipment— the Internet has no single owner. The routers that do the system's heavy lifting, gathering the "data packets" from thousands of smaller networks, reading their address headers, and sending them at high speed to the network's next node, are owned by several major data transfer companies and consortia. These include ANS (owned by the commercial service America OnLine, PSInet, SprintLink, MCI, Pacific Bell and, in Europe, by Eunet and Dante. Some 80 per cent of the Internet's traffic is carried by the three largest Internet service providers: MCI, ANS and Sprint.

Who runs the Internet?

It follows from the lack of a single owner that there is no czar of the Internet who could turn it off tomorrow on a whim, no Internet Senate that could send it careening off in a new direction simply by taking a vote.

The nearest the Internet gets to a manager is the Internet Society. But even this is a series of committees, working groups, and task forces, comprising technical people from government agencies, academic institutions and major service providers. These groups design and accept the technical standards that allow the computers to talk to one another. However, "the society has no coercive power", according to Vinton Cerf, founder and president of the Internet Society, and a senior vice-president at MCI. "Nothing they do is enforceable. It's all enlightened self-interest. The real secret behind the Internet is that it's a grass-roots, bottom-up system."

This becomes evident if you look at how the Internet Society works. The central standards body, the Internet Engineering Task Force (IETF), works online, only meeting face to face three times a year. According to Anthony Rutkowski, executive director of the Internet Society these meetings "bring together more than 500 people at the meeting, with multicasting to more than 600 additional sites around the world".

The number of Internet connections could reach 1.5 million by 2000 and 1.5 billion by 2010.

The IETF also writes software. Members write code, criticise and test new information tools and services, free from stifling formalities. With the growth of the Internet, the scaling of software to cope with the extra volume has become increasingly important. Internet addresses, for example, for local networks (such as "feat.newsci.ipc.co.uk") actually represent 32-bit numerical addresses, much like telephone numbers. But there is a difference. Dialling "011" on any telephone in the US signals that you are making an international call. If the next two digits are "44," you're heading for Britain. If "171" follows, you've got inner London.

Internet addresses, however, are not hierarchical, they are random. Every major Internet router has to carry an enormous "look-up" table with the whereabouts of all 50,000 Internet-addressable networks, and each of these tables must be updated constantly. The society wants to change to a hierarchical scheme, which means changing everyone's address without interrupting service. No small task.

Nor is one of the society's other projects: working on a standardised 128-bit address to accommodate the expected growth in networks connecting to the Internet. Cerf estimates the number of Internet connections could reach 1.5 million by 2000 and 1.5 billion by 2010.

Who pays for the Internet?

Right now, popular commercial systems such as CompuServe, with their chat rooms, databases and conversation forums, charge by the minute. But on the Net itself, you pay for your connection, not for how much you use it. A simple modem service, capable of carrying 14,400 bits per second, might typically cost $200 per year, while the cost of a "T-1" connection for a major university, capable of carrying 1.5 million bits per second, might range from $20,000 to $50,000 per year. The various providers have a "zero settlements" policy—they assume that the service they provide is roughly equal to the service that they receive from other providers. These factors mean that it costs no more to send a note to Auckland or to Osaka than it does to send it across town.

But obviously some uses burden the system more than others. Video conferencing, downloading *Jurassic Park* or a major piece of software, two people working interactively on the same graphics a thousand kilometres apart, or exploring a three-dimensional "virtual world" all use a lot more of the system's resources than sending a note to a friend or logging on to a chat service.

It's in the nature of the Internet that distance is no object.

Most of the new ways of using the Internet are hogs for bandwidth and memory. The World Wide Web, for example, has grown like an arachnophobe's nightmare. This protocol allows people with web browser software to receive information in graphic form (text, tables, charts, pictures, and even audio and video clips) from tens of thousands of sites around the world. Virtually unheard of in 1993, by the beginning of 1995 it had grown to 14 per cent of the total traffic on the Internet. And this is only the start.

"I believe the Web will represent a half of all Internet traffic by the beginning of 1996 because it is the easiest and preferred way of presenting information, either for free or for sale," says Tim Krauskopf, vice-president of research and development at Spyglass, the company that developed the Enhanced Mosaic web browser.

With Web browsing software and new interactive uses, the potential for using graphics and video conferencing becomes real. As Cerf says: "We are worried about interactive video and voice requirements." This means that every part of the system will have to keep upgrading its capacity to provide for these new uses. The switches, for instance, will have to grow from the T-1 (at 1.5 Mbps [megabytes per second]) to T-3s (which at 45 Mbps carry most of today's backbone traffic) or even OC-3s (155 Mbps).

Who will pay for these upgrades? If the Net keeps to its "flat-fee" tradition, everyone will. It is possible that the price of these upgrades will fall so rapidly, and the number of new users willing to pay a monthly fee will rise so fast, that the money will be there. But it is also possible that those monthly fees will have to increase to pay for the new capacity.

Another way of raising the cash is to send people bills based on the strain their choice of applications puts on the network. A version of the Internet's "operating system", TCP/IP IP6, carries a "flow ID", a special line in the header to identify which interactive uses need to go where. This could also be used to charge heavy users more, or even to allow people who want special treatment—to jump to the head of the queue during peak hours, for example—to get it and pay for it without burdening the ordinary user who only sends e-mail and the occasional message on Usenet.

But the problem is incredibly complex. In today's free-wheeling Internet, for instance, I might ask a question of a computer just a few kilometres away. The answer will come back in packets that are "from" that computer and "to" me. How would the software know that it should bill the answer to me, and not to the computer that I interrogated? And the computer that I queried might assemble the answers from computers in Switzerland or Spain, or cause a cascade of actions on other computers that I don't even know about.

One fear voiced in some American newspapers is that . . . competing pressures will lead to the "balkanisation" of the Net.

It's in the nature of the Internet that distance is no object, and that resources are dispersed worldwide in hundreds or thousands of computers rather than held on massive central databases. Wonderfully cheap, efficient and interactive to use, a nightmare to cost.

One way out could lie in novel ways of charging for services. Imagine, for example, a free e-mail service. Dial a toll-free number from anywhere, log on, and send and receive all the messages you want. It won't cost you anything. The only catch is that the e-mail shows up on your screens in envelopes stamped with a corporate logo. Click on the envelope, and you get your message. Click on the logo to find out more about the advertiser, enter contests, or get coupons you can print out and use. This is no fantasy—ProductView Interactive of Cambridge, Massachusetts, has already announced such a service, and advertisers are said to be lining up.

Other services, such as HotWired, the pioneering online magazine, and the Internet publisher, Global Network Navigator, already offer Web pages full of fascinating information, with each page sponsored by a company. The advertisement, at the bottom of the screen, is small but if you click on it, the sponsor's whole catalogue may appear on the screen.

Then there is the Internet Shopping Network, an online, interactive shopping channel, which has been signing up 400 people a day since it opened its doors on 1 April 1995. And over 60 organisations have joined forces under the CommerceNet banner to encourage the growth of an Internet marketplace that will be open, easy-to-use and ready to expand rapidly.

And there are numerous schemes afoot for encryption protocols that will make it possible to transfer money—safely and securely—across the

Internet. Some network providers and advertisers have developed software that can log the record of where users wander, "clickstreams" which show the pattern of their online interests so advertisers can target them with offers that they won't want to refuse. At a conference, Scott Mc-Nealy, the chairman of Sun Microsystems, predicted: "Within the next few years, business-to-consumer electronic commerce could begin to replace much of the world's existing business infrastructure."

Future directions for the Internet

One fear voiced in some American newspapers is that these competing pressures will lead to the "balkanisation" of the Net. But Varian disagrees: "I don't think it will come to that, since so many people have come to depend on it. There is such an economic advantage to being able to talk to each other, it's hard to see how the competitors could leave that money on the table." This view is backed up by the Internet Society's Rutkowski. "The greatest value of the public Internet is its connectivity. Virtually everyone understands that."

Another scenario is what people are calling the "hacker's dream". The price of everything falls so rapidly and the efficiencies of the architecture are so great that the technology needed to use the Internet becomes nearly free. Large commercial enterprises keep to their own cybermalls, leaving the rest of cyberspace unpaved. A free-floating cybercash economy develops which has no connection with the Earth-bound banking system. The Internet evolves as a self-organising, smoothly functioning anarchy. Rutkowski calls this "an extreme that has elements of the plausible".

The flip side is the Internet as cyberspace version of a gargantuan shopping mall, dominated by big companies. In this vision, the Net is thoroughly commercialised, produced by professionals, and carries a charge, or advertising or both. Publishing information on the Internet becomes so expensive that free or nearly free access to it by individuals almost ceases to exist.

> *The cybermall may be able to coexist with the dreams of hackers.*

David Wetherell, chief executive officer of Booklink Technologies in Wilmington, Massachusetts, a company that develops software for navigating the Internet, finds this scenario worrying. "The great thing about the Internet today is that no one owns it. If you have a good product or service, you can put it up on the network and let the public decide if it's good."

Wetherell is not alone in his concern. Business and marketing experts such as Donna Hoffman, a professor at Vanderbilt University in Tennessee and specialist on the new media, fear that Microsoft and other major companies will attempt to dominate the Internet, building toll booths up and down the information highway and turning it into yet another broadcast medium.

On the other hand, science writer Barry Shell, though a critic of corporate intrusion on the Net, is not too worried: "The Internet, with its open, distributed structure, was designed to withstand a nuclear attack. If it can do that, it can withstand corporate America."

Another joker in the futures pack is unlimited bandwidth. There are no limitations, unlike the open land around a city. In cyberspace you can always make more space, provided the technology continues on the course it has taken over the past two decades. The cybermall may be able to coexist with the dreams of hackers. As Rutkowski describes this scenario, "diversity—much like the real world, only much more accessible".

Varian agrees. "If you build a system robust enough to handle interactive video, everything else is free, essentially. All the more traditional applications, such as e-mail and file transfer, can just go along for the ride because their demands for bandwidth are so much smaller." How realistic this is depends on the freedom given to the software developers designing for the Internet.

Many bottlenecks

There are many bottlenecks on the future of the Internet. The US National Security Agency, for instance, has for years been battling to suppress the use of "unbreakable" public-key cryptography online, and a grand jury in California's Silicon Valley [considered but declined] to bring criminal charges against cryptography pioneer Phil Zimmerman for allowing his PGP (Pretty Good Privacy) cryptography program to escape onto the Internet.

The goal of the NSA and some ocher elements of the US government (and indeed a number of other governments) is to force all Net cryptography programs to have "trapdoors" that are accessible by law enforcement agents. Yet such trapdoors mean that hackers will be able to break into the software and will greatly reduce the willingness of business and commercial users to trust it with commercial secrets, credit-card numbers, and financial transfers.

Other governments fear the freedom that the Internet gives its users. The Net's highly distributed nature makes restrictions and regulations fundamentally difficult to enforce. Yet its role as a potentially powerful engine of economic development means that these governments cannot afford to simply ban it.

Many believe [the Internet] will be one of the most powerful shapers of the 21st century.

The Chinese government, for instance, realises that it must allow the Internet into China because it represents the technological future. Yet the country's rulers fear the free flow of information and debate it will bring. As a compromise, the government has set an artificially high price on Internet access in a bid to restrict the number of people who can use the Internet.

And other totalitarian governments around the world such as that of Singapore have set various restrictions on its use.

Ironically, what could limit the growth and usefulness of the Internet is its very power. A technology that can bring all the information from everywhere to your own computer is useless unless it can also help you find what you really want, the people that you want to talk to, and the conversation that you want to join. So a crucial test of the viability of the Internet will be the development of filters for all that information: software agents, mail handlers and human intermediaries such as Net searchers, conference moderators and digest editors.

A powerful point of view is fast becoming a valuable commodity: what does the world of the Internet look like through [U.S. House of Representatives Speaker] Newt Gingrich's eyes? Or [South African president] Nelson Mandela's? It will be possible to make a living as a "host" or "lens" on the Internet, not by selling your own writings, but by selling your own point of view about what is interesting, important and imperative to know.

If the Internet struggles past the bottlenecks of excess regulation and excess information, many believe it will be one of the most powerful shapers of the 21st century.

Rutkowski speaks of it as "a fundamental transformation", an entire information infrastructure built from the bottom up, a "robust global mesh" of computers that allows "open collaboration in the hyperdevelopment and evolution of new technologies" and one that will "transform the structure, methods and individual skills within enterprises, institutions, and professions of all kinds. . . . A hundred years from now, history may well record the emergence and implementation of the Internet protocol as a profound turning point in the evolution of human communication—of much greater significance than the creation of the printing press."

2

The Information Superhighway Will Offer Many Benefits

United States Advisory Council on the
National Information Infrastructure

*The United States Advisory Council on the National Information Infra-
structure is an ad hoc committee formed by President Bill Clinton in
1993.*

The Information Superhighway is a growing infrastructure of people, technologies, and content. The United States will reap many
benefits from the Information Superhighway, which will fundamentally change the nation's institutions, including business, education, government, and health care. Besides bringing economic,
educational, and employment benefits, the products and services
available via the Information Superhighway will vastly improve
the quality and convenience of everyday life.

The United States stands today in the midst of one of the great revolu-
tions in recorded history: the Information Age. This revolution is
changing fundamentally the ways in which people work, learn, communicate, care for their own health, and create their home lives.

The revolution is already bringing about fundamental structural
changes in the pivotal institutions of contemporary life. The benefits of
the Information Superhighway are apparent, especially in the areas of education and lifelong learning, and opportunities for economic growth.

As Americans continue the challenging and exciting task of designing
and implementing the Information Superhighway for the next millennium, the U.S. Advisory Council on the Information Infrastructure urges
that the Nation adopt five fundamental goals, discussed in the section on
the Council's Vision.

As the Nation strives to attain the goals of the Information Superhighway, key policy issues, such as the appropriate role of the private sec-

United States Advisory Council on the National Information Infrastructure, "America on the
Information Superhighway," in *A Nation of Opportunity: A Final Report of the United States Advisory
Council on the National Information Infrastructure*, Washington, D.C., January 1996.

tor and government, constitutional rights and freedoms, the need to protect intellectual property, and role of universal access, must be addressed.

The revolution is affecting how business manufactures and distributes goods and services, how government serves the public, how health care institutions care for their patients, how schools educate young people and adults, and ultimately how we participate in our democratic society.

But is this amazing new development altogether a good thing? Certainly, the Council believes that it has the potential to improve substantially the quality of life.

Benefits of the Information Superhighway

The Information Superhighway is more than the Internet. It is a series of components, including the collection of public and private high-speed, interactive, narrow, and broadband networks that exist today and will emerge tomorrow.

- It is the satellite, terrestrial, and wireless technologies that deliver content to homes, businesses, and other public and private institutions.
- It is the information and content that flow over the infrastructure, whether in the form of databases, the written word, a film, a piece of music, a sound recording, a picture, or computer software.
- It is the computers, televisions, telephones, radios, and other products that people will employ to access the infrastructure.
- It is the people who will provide, manage, and generate new information, and those who will help others to do the same.
- And it is the individual Americans who will use and benefit from the Information Superhighway.

The Information Superhighway is a term that encompasses all these components and captures the vision of a nationwide, invisible, seamless, dynamic web of transmission mechanisms, information, appliances, content, and people.

The Information Superhighway already offers dozens of new products and services that will greatly improve the overall quality and convenience of our everyday lives.

The U.S. economy has long been among the most competitive in the world. As information increasingly becomes the currency of economic strength, the Information Superhighway promises enormous economic benefits, in terms of productivity and our ability to compete in the new global marketplace. In 1995, and for the second year running, the United States was ranked the world's most competitive economy—due in no small part to our unique ability to use computers and telecommunications to make our information work harder and travel faster.

At home, this translates into unprecedented opportunities to advance our social progress and improve the living standards and quality of life for all Americans. These benefits, however, will depend more than ever before on educational achievement. The Information Superhighway is already helping prepare Americans for this future by both improving the quality of our educational system and making educational opportunities more accessible to people of all ages and in all geographic locations.

Education and lifelong learning

In our Nation's classrooms, the Information Superhighway is being used to substantially improve the quality of general and technical education that our children receive. Real-time interactive video, audio, and data networks are now supplementing classroom resources and allowing students to draw on the knowledge of myriad, geographically dispersed educators and experts.

Further, students are increasingly able to interact electronically with their peers at schools in other regions of the country—exchanging knowledge, values, and cultures. Demonstration projects that currently employ this technology in some of our Nation's most economically disadvantaged classrooms reveal dramatic improvements in learning.

Using the Information Superhighway of the twenty-first century, all our schoolchildren—whatever their geographic location or socioeconomic background—also will have electronic access to the educational resources of our most prestigious libraries. They will be digital libraries, featuring the next generation of online multimedia databases that will allow a bulky Sunday newspaper to be downloaded in just seconds.

Similar access to education is transforming the workplace, where the desktop PC enables workers to draw on such diverse resources as online multimedia networks and live, interactive video conferences. From earning a master's degree or doctorate to receiving new product training, employees will increasingly come to rely on the Information Superhighway to further their career goals.

Economic growth

Beyond these essentials—enhanced economic, educational, and employment benefits—the Information Superhighway already offers dozens of new products and services that will greatly improve the overall quality and convenience of our everyday lives.

Already through today's existing telecommunication infrastructure, we can catch a glimpse of the many benefits that await us. Automated teller machines (ATMs) give us instant access to cash—anytime and almost anywhere. Cable TV and today's newest, small-dish satellite TV antennas put a virtual entertainment cornucopia in our living rooms. Cellular phones keep us in touch—whenever, wherever we want to be. Electronic networks, including the World Wide Web, provide access to a broad variety of information and resources.

Through the Information Superhighway, the nature of work process is changing dramatically, becoming more inclusive and more collaborative. Workers will be able to draw upon the diverse ideas and expertise of geographically and culturally disparate participants. If people are tied to the home by family commitments, personal preference, or other reasons, "telecommuting" will give them full access to the workplace.

Small businesses are actively contributing to development of the Information Superhighway. They are in turn likely to benefit significantly from the electronic expansion of market and other opportunities.

In conclusion, the Information Superhighway we envision holds vast potential to offer this Nation and its people unlimited opportunities for economic growth, social progress, and cultural understanding. Moreover, by facilitating universal participation in every aspect of American society, the Information Superhighway will enable us to maximize the value of all our human resources, revitalize our Nation's social and economic fabric, and reaffirm our country's sense of community.

The council's vision

As we Americans continue the challenging and exciting task of designing and implementing the Information Superhighway for the next millennium, the Council urges that the Nation adopt the following five fundamental goals.

First, let us find ways to make information technology work for us, the people of this country, by ensuring that these wondrous new resources advance American constitutional precepts, our diverse cultural values, and our sense of equity.

Second, let us ensure, too, that getting America online results in stronger communities, and a stronger sense of national community.

Third, let us extend to every person in every community the opportunity to participate in building the Information Superhighway. The Information Superhighway must be a tool that is available to all Americans—people of all ages, those from a wide range of economic, social, and cultural backgrounds, and those with a wide range of functional abilities and limitations—not just a select few. It must be affordable, easy to use, and accessible from even the most disadvantaged neighborhood or remote dwelling.

Fourth, let us ensure that we Americans take responsibility for the building of the Superhighway—private sector, government at all levels, and individuals.

And, fifth, let us maintain our world leadership in developing the services, products, and an open and competitive market that lead to deployment of the Information Superhighway. Research and development will be an essential component of its sustained evolution.

Importantly, the enhanced Information Superhighway we construct also will serve as our on-ramp to the Global Information Superhighway—the fast-emerging international marketplace of commerce, information, and ideas. By invoking the energies and ingenuity of the private sector, this country can greatly improve the levels of education, standard of living, and economic future of its people—and become a supplier to the world as other countries mount their own efforts to join the Global Information Superhighway.

3

The Internet Will Improve Education

Andy Carvin

Andy Carvin is an education and information technology specialist for the Corporation for Public Broadcasting in Washington, D.C. He created and maintains EdWeb: Exploring Technology and School Reform, *an evolving "hyperbook" available on the World Wide Web.*

Students learn more effectively when they become actively engaged in the educational process, particularly when the interactivity of classroom computers and the World Wide Web is involved. The growth of the Web and the emergence of new hypermedia tools promise to make the Internet an innovative learning medium that will provide students with an abundance of documents and resources. Such potential to improve education can be better met if volunteers and computer professionals offer their services to help classrooms access the Internet.

The advent of the World Wide Web comes at an exciting, yet controversial juncture in American education reform. Though more detailed information on education reform policy can be found elsewhere on EdWeb, certain basic trends and terms should be mentioned briefly. Possibly the most important point that must be addressed is the current emphasis towards interactivity in the learning process. The term "interactivity" has become somewhat of a buzzword in American pop culture, education and commerce—for example, some software packages attempt to add to their appeal by emphasizing the product's "interactive" nature. In other words, passive learning doesn't work, yet interactive learning works wonders.

Yet beyond all of the hype and rhetoric surrounding interactivity in education, there is a solid backdrop of empirical analysis to support the positive nature of interactive learning. Simply put, students of all ages learn better when they are actively engaged in a process, whether that process comes in the form of a sophisticated multimedia package or a low-tech classroom debate on current events. Over the years, social sci-

From Andy Carvin, "A New Tool in the Arsenal: The Role of the Web in Curricular Reform" and "Conclusion: What Next for the Web and Education?" part of "The World Wide Web in Education: A Closer Look," in his hyperbook *EdWeb: Exploring Technology and School Reform.*

entists and education researchers have attempted with reasonable success to debunk the traditional notion of the passive classroom environment. But considering the nature of that notion—one teacher lecturing to a large class, encouraging informational absorption and regurgitation, and finally assessing the students by a series of simplistic standardized tests—it doesn't take a reformer with a PhD in educational psychology to recognize that the old ways of teaching and learning need some serious restructuring. In order for today's young people to become competitive in tomorrow's marketplace, yesterday's pedagogical methodology is no longer enough.

Encouraging student interest

One of the key problems in education reform is that traditional teaching fails because students have no use or interest in much of the material as it is presented, yet in order to expand their understanding of a given subject, they must become involved in the entire teaching process. For example, producing a physics experiment in order to actively discover the results, in addition to exploring the social context in which the original experiment was performed, has more educational value than merely hearing a lecture about how some scientist first attempted the experiment several centuries ago.

Engaging students from a variety of angles and allowing them to feel as if they are a part of the subject matter will often lead to them becoming more interested in (or at least more willing to discuss) that subject. Therefore, they invest more mental energy and thus commit the concept to memory with a better comprehensive understanding of it. Roger Schank of Northwestern University's Institute of the Learning Sciences proposes that learning be attained through the use of goal-based scenarios—the teacher, with a set of learning goals in hand, allows the students to explore the subject from their own particular point of view. Students, when encouraged and given the proper opportunity and medium, can express a wealth of opinions on nearly any subject. And by giving them the chance to articulate and share their thoughts, they can grasp the meaning of the subject and thus understand it better.

No passing fad

Though there are some technoskeptics and informational Luddites who suggest that the World Wide Web is only a passing fad, certain facts would suggest that this is highly unlikely. The Web has found enormous success word-of-mouth—it is soon expected to pass file transfer protocol [FTP] as the highest user of bandwidth on the Internet. Moreover, commercial developers have recently adopted the Web as their new pet cybermedium, from the Star Trek: Voyager site to Time/Warner's Pathfinder. Increasing the profitability of these ventures are the planned inclusions of basic Web browsers in the operating systems for both Macintosh and Intel-based PCs, as well as Prodigy's and America Online's moves to make the Web accessible over its commercial subscription services to millions of users.

Assuming that the future of the Web is secure, at least for several years to come, what steps must be taken in order to further its development as an educational instrument? Above all else, institutional access to the Internet must increase dramatically. Though many schools are lucky enough to have formed partnerships with universities and local business in order to gain access (and still others have received networking grants or employ persistent technophiles as educators), the overwhelming majority of schools lack the hardware needed just to get connected in the first place. And while policymakers and politicians argue how to best finance schools for technology development, it is still possible for many schools to get started.

Ideally, more community networks and freenets must begin to offer Web access at reasonable rates, and more importantly, they must offer schools and classrooms server accounts so they may publish Web sites of their own. The Web will only grow if people are willing to commit the time and energy to creative pursuits, and the first step to this goal will always be through the providing of easy access. Additionally, members of the community who already have access and experience should offer their assistance to demonstrating to others what the Web can do and how simple it is to develop a new site. In the world of Web development, there are scores of experts who are always willing to donate their time to each other in order to expand the various offerings already available over the Web.

Teachers and students alike will be able to explore cyberspace and design new resources for a multitude of purposes that have yet to be realized.

Yet because of the communal nature of the Internet, rarely do we see them venturing out of cyberspace into the real world to provide their knowledge to those who lack it. This is not to say that there aren't committed individuals who are doing more than their fair share to enhance the educational community, but the numbers of volunteers must increase if we ever truly wish to see the Web expand into education. And as people begin to explore the Web and publish their own electronic products, the quality and creativity of Web sites will increase dramatically. Few Web sites ever exist in a vacuum—as people access it, the publisher is bound to get inundated with suggestions, criticism, and encouragement, which usually translate into further development of the site.

What is bound to be most fascinating, though, is the integration of new Internet technologies into the world of the Web. For instance, Internet Relay Chats (real-time group discussions) and MUD's (Multiple User Dungeons, essentially an IRC in an interesting setting) could provide users and designers with the ability to interact with each other live, instead of having to wait for a listserv to distribute the information as it is posted via e-mail. Similarly, webmasters may begin to integrate the user of CUSeeMe into Web sites. CUSeeMe, a teleconferencing program developed at Cornell, allows users to see and hear each other by way of a video camera by converting the data into an Internet-compatible format. Programmers are now experimenting with software that will allow easy access to these live discussions in a Web environment, and when combined with the Web's audiovisual capabilities, one could only begin to imagine the possibilities for on-line education and enhancement.

And what of the next generation of hypermedia tools—is there a protocol which will be better than the Web? According to some Internauts, there already is. Hyper-G, a new protocol designed by researchers in Austria, is a cross between the Web and gopher. Like the Web, Hyper-G is easily hypernavigatable and can access other Internet tools like FTP and e-mail. But unlike the Web, Hyper-G can handle enormous amounts of data and automatically process it into multiple subject areas. It can interpret Postscript files, which saves time and allows greater flexibility in terms of document layout. Perhaps most interesting is Hyper-G's ability to assign users access privileges, so users can get on and add their own documents to certain areas and thus become telecommuting co-publishers of a site. Fortunately for proponents of the World Wide Web, Hyper-G is totally compatible with Web browsers and vice-versa, so as Hyper-G begins to spread throughout the Internet, its high-data advantages will probably steer it towards certain uses. In the end, it will not be a matter of Hyper-G versus the Web; more likely is that they will complement each other as people begin to explore each protocol's potential.

But for now, the World Wide Web will continue as the protocol of choice for many network users, and its growth as an education tool will doubtfully taper off any time soon. The Web is accepted internationally because of its relative ease of use and cross-compatibility, and future changes in HTML standards (especially in layout design and in the integration of live communication protocols) will inevitably make it even more powerful. For the educational community, on-line hypermedia offers a simple way to design interactive lessons for local and distant use. And as the World Wide Web becomes more accessible to schools around the country, teachers and students alike will be able to explore cyberspace and design new resources for a multitude of purposes that have yet to be realized.

4

Internet Commerce
Is Poised to Flourish

Debora Spar and Jeffrey J. Bussgang

Debora Spar is an associate professor at Harvard University School of Business in Boston. Jeffrey J. Bussgang is the director of transaction products for Open Market, a Cambridge, Massachusetts, computer software company.

The commercial potential of the Internet is vast, but business in cyberspace is risky for many companies because few rules currently govern commerce there. In order to ensure that business can be conducted in an orderly, effective manner, rules must be created. Access providers and business communities can play a large role in establishing and enforcing guidelines for protecting property rights, governing currency, and securing information on the Internet. These measures would guarantee that business on the Internet will be efficient and profitable.

E ver since the Internet burst into the public realm, it has held aloft the promise of a commercial revolution. The promise is of a radical new world of business—a friction-free arena where millions of buyers and sellers complete their transactions cheaply, instantaneously, and anonymously. Cut free from layers of middlemen, companies will be able to sell their products directly to their customers; consumers will be able to customize products, interact with the companies that supply them, and conduct business from the comfort of their own homes. By bringing companies and customers together, the Internet thus promises to widen markets, increase efficiencies, and lower costs. Those are radical promises, and on their strength thousands of companies have already joined a massive scramble to cyberspace.

For many of those companies, however, the Internet has yet to deliver on its promises. Although doing business in cyberspace may be novel and exhilarating, it can also be frustrating, confusing, and even unprofitable. Whereas for some companies on-line commerce is a natural outgrowth of their business, for others—particularly in information-

Reprinted by permission of *Harvard Business Review*. "Ruling the Net" by Debora Spar and Jeffrey J. Bussgang, May/June 1996. Copyright ©1996 by the President and Fellows of Harvard College; all rights reserved.

intensive industries such as software, publishing, and financial services—moving into cyberspace is a difficult endeavor. The problems these companies face have little to do with a lack of technology or imagination. They stem instead from a lack of rules.

Why, in the midst of such a critical transformation, should managers pause to consider anything so mundane as rules? The answer is that rules are critical to commerce. Without the order that rules create, business cannot be conducted.

A lack of rules

At the moment, there are few rules in cyberspace. The legal status of electronic copyright is still vague, as are the legal and practical issues surrounding on-line exchange and "electronic cash." There is also limited authority to enforce rules on the Internet and little capacity to punish those who violate the norms of on-line conduct. Although these problems have been well documented, they persist nevertheless. And until they are solved, cyberspace will remain a frontier town—a land of opportunities, to be sure, but also one of tremendous risks.

In surveying this frontier, it is important to realize that the current lack of rules does not necessarily mean that governments will send in the cavalry or that companies will walk away in despair, leaving the Internet to the hackers and the chat lines. Instead, it simply means that companies need to think carefully before making any headlong leaps into cyberspace. Rather than just posting pages on the World Wide Web, for instance, companies may want to move more selectively, clustering themselves into on-line communities where rules prevail and commerce can proceed. Auto parts suppliers, for example, might band together in an exclusive network serving only the auto industry, whereas investment management firms might want to sell their services only where distribution is limited and payment ensured.

These sorts of on-line communities will create a very different form of electronic commerce from the one envisioned today by many Internet adherents. The communities will not be open to all; they will increasingly charge customers for their services; and they will not permit information to flow across seamless borders. They will change the current spirit of the Internet and bring order and management to the Net's unruly tangle. By writing the rules for commercial transactions, on-line communities will also shift the balance of power between business and government toward business. That evolution will occur not because of the power of particular companies, or because business is opposed by nature to an open Internet or a free flow of information. Rather, commerce will move toward on-line communities simply because companies need a basic infrastructure of rules to survive.

This vision of Internet commerce is a less radical one than that embraced by many Internet proponents, and a far cry from the friction-free world of open and unregulated commerce espoused by such figures as [Microsoft founder and chairman] Bill Gates. But it takes into account the realities facing most companies today. In our view, the commercial promise of the Internet is still vast, but it does not lie in the unmanaged reaches of cyberspace. Nor does it come solely from the Internet's technical ability to facilitate transactions and reduce costs. Instead, the promise lies in the ability of companies to form well-defined communities that will protect their property and promote their own interests. It lies in the potential of other companies to construct these communities, to intermediate their commerce, and to guard their members. The commercial promise of the Internet, in short, requires rules for its fulfillment. And the companies that stand to reap the greatest profits in cyberspace are the pioneers who will write, support, and enforce the new rules of the emerging frontier.

The rules of exchange

When the Internet was first developed in the 1960s, it was governed by clear codes of conduct and working norms of behavior. Developed by a community of like-minded scientists, the rules were rarely written down or even explicit, but they did not have to be, because travelers on the Net could easily observe them. Just as early automobile drivers informally devised rules of the road, so too did early Internet users develop their own norms of behavior. They created symbols to express emotions such as happiness [:-)] and unhappiness [:-(]. They created some explicit rules, such as Don't change the subject and Read the FAQ [frequently-asked-questions] file, and they even created a language of sorts with terms such as *flame* and *spam*. Despite its outward image as an untamed realm of hackers, the early Net was in fact a rule-bound, orderly community. The rules, however, evolved to serve the interests of a particular community—researchers in academia and in the U.S. Department of Defense, who had no desire to profit from their on-line activities.

For roughly 20 years, that community flourished. But in the early 1990s, the community's rules and values were suddenly attacked by hordes of "newbies," new users who had scrambled on-line. Whereas the Internet in the early 1980s consisted of only about 25 linked networks, it had grown by 1995 to include more than 44,000 networks extending to 160 countries and including 26,000 registered commercial entities. Somewhere between 40 million and 50 million computers were connected to Internet hosts in 1995, and that number was growing by an estimated 10% to 20% per month.

The [Internet's commercial] promise lies in the ability of companies to form well-defined communities that will protect their property and promote their own interests.

The entrance of the newbies did more than just increase the sheer numbers on the Internet; it led to a fundamental change in the Net's culture. Arriving on-line largely through new commercial services and Internet access providers, these new users were riding a wave of privatization that began with the emergence of commercial service providers in 1989 and continued when the Internet was officially opened to commercial ventures in 1990. The newbies had little interest in the research questions that had previously bound users together. They were also largely unfamiliar with many of the Internet's specific protocols. Cyberspace for the newbies was simply an adventure—an opportunity to meet people, gain information, and perhaps re-create some sense of small-town intimacy and immediacy. But many newcomers also came to cyberspace for profit, to explore the Net's potential, and to stake a claim in a technology that promised to revolutionize the nature of transactions. As a result, the Internet's new business district—the ".com domain"—quickly swelled to become the largest sector of the Net.

Dramatic levels of growth and a radical shift in the Internet's population of users make necessary a new set of on-line rules. Yet because the Net lacks any central authority or organizing structure, rules are emerging piecemeal, pulled and prodded by the often conflicting interests of business, governmental agencies, and traditional Net users. In general, the governmental agencies and traditional users have been more explicit than businesses in describing how they want rules to evolve. The U.S. government, for example, has focused largely on safeguarding defense-related access and regulating access to pornography. Traditional users have lobbied vociferously for open communications, universal access, and a ban on government intervention of any sort. The business community, by contrast, has been relatively quiet. Rather than thinking abstractly about rules, most companies have concentrated on the more immediate tasks of getting on-line and claiming a stake in cyberspace.

That focus is shortsighted because it overlooks the greatest potential for companies on the Internet: the opportunity not only to master the game of electronic commerce but also to create the rules of the game. In particular, companies can influence the creation of rules in three distinct areas: property rights, means of exchange, and enforcement.

Property rights

All economic systems are based fundamentally on a shared understanding of property rights. Developed over decades or even centuries, property rights clarify the basis of ownership and exchange. They provide a consistent way of defining who owns what and how possessions can be transferred from one owner to another. Property rights reduce the costs of exchange by clarifying ownership and providing a means for punishing thieves; thus they define not only possession but also theft.

In modern market economies, property rights also provide the incentives that drive growth. If property is communal or property rights are ill defined, no one in the community has much incentive to produce anything more than he or she can consume. What creates the incentive and impels progress is a system that defines private property and enables its owners to make use of it for their own benefit. Without the ability to garner the returns from one's property, there is no incentive to invest in specialization or technology or even to put in a hard day's work. To generate such investments, communities create and preserve rules of private property.[1] And as economies evolve, so too must the rules.

The connection between property rights and commerce applies with full force to the Internet. The advent of electronic commerce does not eliminate business's basic need for an infrastructure to clarify ownership and allow owners to reap economic rewards. But at the moment, on-line property rights are imprecisely defined; the Net remains a virtual free-for-all where information is seen as a public good and ownership is up for grabs.

Understandably, then, companies that deal in the business of information are approaching the Net with caution. The Recording Industry Association of America, for instance, held back because it was worried that its products might be changed or misrepresented on-line. Likewise, the Smithsonian Institution has limited the electronic reproduction of its artistic works; as a spokesperson told the *New York Times*, the institution reasons that "at least for now . . . cyberspace is a chaotic wild west frontier full of highway bandits and subject to only the roughest kind of vigilante justice."

By guaranteeing the rights of intellectual property owners, copyright law should allow information-based companies to move more confidently onto the Internet.

There is one fairly obvious way to solve the problem of property rights on the Internet: the creation of law by central governments. In cyberspace, that law would probably come from an extension of existing copyright law. Because copyright provides for the commercialization of intangible products—intellectual property—the extension of copyright law into cyberspace would seem to make sense. By guaranteeing the rights of intellectual property owners, copyright law should allow information-based companies to move more confidently onto the Internet. Accordingly, lawmakers in Washington, D.C., have recently begun to tinker with copyright law. In September 1995, a group convened by the White House's Information Infrastructure Task Force recommended changing the 1976 copyright law to explicitly include transmission as a form of distribution. The group also endorsed a "fair use" provision that would limit any noncommercial use of intellectual property that nevertheless damages the legal owner of the property.

If enacted as law, these provisions will do a lot to protect the property of companies that transact in cyberspace. But they won't do nearly enough. First, copyright is already one of the most intricate and esoteric areas of law. Courts vary widely in their interpretation of existing statutes and even in their understanding of a given law's intent. The extension of those laws into a new realm of commerce is almost sure to create ambiguity and uncertainty, leaving courts and litigants to fumble toward new definitions of private property and property rights. Second, because the laws are national, they will have little influence on the Internet's international transactions. Thus, even if the laws stop a company based in Cincinnati from covertly downloading a competitor's software, textbook, or database, they may not stop that company from routing the material through a computer in Thailand or the Netherlands. Finally, even if the laws were applied at the global level (and there is some talk of doing so under the World Trade Organization), they still would not provide the means for businesses to determine if their information has been altered or copied in cyberspace. The laws also offer no solution to the thorny problems involved in tracing on-line violations. Even if a company suspects that its product has been stolen, how can it find the thief, especially if the transactions have been routed through multiple sites and untraceable user IDs?

Again, there are measures that governments can take to fill those gaps. They can establish a central registration point for user IDs, as France initially did with its innovative Minitel service. They can use central crime-fighting units, as the United States did in directing a raid by the FBI on on-line pornography and in tracking down Kevin Mitnick, the credit card hacker. But such forays are likely to be limited both by the diffuse structure of the Internet and by the antigovernment sentiment that still prevails within it.

Meanwhile, the door is open for private companies to move directly into the rule-making business. Although companies cannot write the rules of intellectual property rights, they can establish rule-bound areas of the Internet—"virtual communities" in which rules are enforced. In those areas, companies can perform the functions that governments are not yet capable of fulfilling. For a fee or by contract, they can protect the rights of on-line property. Just as merchants in medieval times developed the customs and practices that eventually became commercial law in Europe, so can contemporary companies and entrepreneurs create the rules of electronic commerce.

Consider, for example, the services provided by America Online. AOL sells access to the Internet. It gives users an easy way to enter cyberspace and a new forum in which to advertise products or disseminate ideas. When new subscribers join AOL, though, they get much more than a pathway to the Net. They get a well-regulated, well-maintained road. AOL offers a user-friendly environment and direct access to commercial services. In return, it regulates all users and demands that they comply with explicit rules. Likewise, when a content provider signs on with AOL, it does not simply transmit its information into the vast reaches of the Internet. Rather, it provides its content—news stories, photographs, flight schedules—directly to AOL, which then redistributes the content to its own subscribers, a discrete and identifiable customer base. By intermediating the transaction, AOL converts the Internet from an open, lawless realm into a secure community where access is controlled and rules are enforced. As a result, AOL can assure its content providers that their sales will be controlled, identified, and reimbursed. In effect, AOL creates and enforces the property rights of its customers. Even without a well-defined legal infrastructure, AOL is writing the rules of commerce.

Means of exchange

Rules for commercial transactions constitute a second area ripe for private intervention. In most economic systems, currency of one form or another is used as payment in transactions. Typically, currency is issued by a central government that retains a monopoly over its creation and backs it with fractional reserves of precious metals or other countries' currencies. Even when the currency is not directly backed by a tangible asset, a government's management of its supply can create value based on confidence (that the government will always accept it as a store of value) and scarcity (because there is never quite enough to go around).

In contrast to the rules of property rights, which must change to meet the demands of electronic commerce, the rules governing currency could probably function quite well for electronic exchange. Even in cyberspace, customers can order goods priced in dollars, charge them to a credit card, and let banks intermediate the financial transaction. There is nothing intrinsic about the Internet that demands new means of exchange. There are no technical obstacles to routing and recording even nontraditional transactions through established routes; nor are there demands for new levels of financial oversight or regulation.

The rules governing currency could probably function quite well for electronic exchange.

Instead, the impetus for change stems from the instantaneous and intangible nature of electronic transactions. If electronic purchases become commonplace, they are likely to include such "microtransactions" as buying one article from the *Atlantic Monthly* or browsing through the *New York Times* for three minutes. The cost of processing those services by credit card would overwhelm the price of the service itself; such costs could doom small on-line entrepreneurs from the start. If payment could take place instantly, however, then the costs of transacting would plummet and commercial activity could flourish. As an added benefit, electronic exchange could, like cash transactions, allow buyers and sellers to maintain their anonymity. With a wallet full of "E-cash," buyers could purchase items quickly and anonymously in cyberspace. Without having to rely on credit cards, bank tellers, and checkbooks, they could save both time and money. This is the radical vision of Internet commerce—fast, cheap, and anonymous.

Technologically, the creation of electronic money depends on the issuance of an anonymous electronic note. An institution would sell electronic money to its customers, coding the E-cash onto a wallet-sized card or transmitting it directly to another on-line merchant. It would debit the disbursed E-money, plus a small transaction fee, from customers' regular bank accounts. For this process to work, the electronic transfers must remain anonymous and secure, and transaction fees must be kept low. In the past, similar requirements were met by the agencies of a central government. Governments printed currency, allowed it to circulate anonymously, punished those who stole or copied it, and covered their expenses through taxation. On the Internet, however, there is no central authority to establish the means of exchange. And national governments have little interest in taking on the problem, because E-cash raises a host of troubling law-enforcement questions. For example, would E-cash expand the possibilities for tax evasion and money laundering? And how would governments track the assets of individuals or the trading balances of states? If E-cash proliferates, many aspects of economic activity will likely escape the scrutiny of government agencies; thus they have little incentive to play any role in its creation.

For private companies, by contrast, the incentives are vast. First, there is the cost-cutting potential of electronic payment. Banks in particular have a considerable interest in cutting the costs of intermediate transactions and moving directly to electronic payment systems. Several institutions, such as Citibank and Wells Fargo, already employ proprietary software systems that allow customers to do their banking on-line. As banks and other financial-service institutions increasingly compete on the basis of transactions rather than relationships, these payment systems will become critical to their success.

But the real breakthrough will come when electronic payment systems are pushed into the broader reaches of cyberspace. Eventually, the value of E-cash, like the value of any currency, will be determined by the market's demand for it. For demand to increase, the currency will have to be widely accepted. In the past, governments ensured this acceptance simply by proclaiming their currency legal tender. In the future, the game will be inherently more competitive. Companies that establish the most accessible and secure means of exchange will capture the market of all those seeking to conduct electronic transactions. And success in this game will breed more success, because a currency's acceptance by some users will increase its attractiveness to others.

The race to develop the means of secure electronic exchange has become one of the most spirited competitions in cyberspace.

Not surprisingly, then, the race to develop the means of secure electronic exchange has become one of the most spirited competitions in cyberspace, with start-ups such as DigiCash and CyberCash taking on established players such as Visa and MasterCard. To some extent, it is a race of technology: Winning will entail the refinement of encryption algorithms—which scramble electronic signals and allow access through mathematically encoded digital signatures—as well as the development of secure "electronic wallets." The race, however, is also about rules, because technology alone cannot support a full-fledged system of electronic exchange. If payment systems are to proliferate along the Internet, some trusted entity will have to oversee and regulate their use. The issue goes beyond the widely publicized threat of credit card theft. The question is, Can large companies attain the confidence necessary to conduct business over the Internet? Even with major leaps in encryption technology, few institutions are likely to feel sufficiently comfortable with the Internet's open architecture to entrust it with millions of dollars' worth of transactions. Performing commercial transactions in a private electronic network is a far cry from allowing them to occur in the blatant public spaces of the Internet.

If companies are to push their financial transactions into the broader reaches of the Net, they will need some means of recourse. At a minimum, they will need to know that some identifiable, credible entity is backing the security of their transactions and preventing widespread fraud and abuse. Historically, governments have served in that role, but private companies will have to do so on the Internet. Financial institutions, with their combination of trusted brand-name and risk-management experience, are particularly well suited for this role. Yet the attributes of those institutions could also eventually adhere to any other trusted entity—the local telephone company, a utility, a local newspaper. In any case, the entity managing an exchange system would also need to bundle its means of exchange with rules of security and enforcement.

Security and enforcement

Security and enforcement pose the most obvious problems for Internet commerce. They also create the most tantalizing opportunities for new business development. Before any E-cash changes hands, and indeed before any real financial transaction occurs on-line, the parties to an exchange must have confidence that their transaction is secure. That is, they must know that the buyers or sellers are really who they claim to be, that the information being exchanged cannot be stolen or altered en route, and that the payment being offered is real.

These levels of security do not yet exist broadly on the Internet. Instead, as information travels through the network, it passes through many computers and sorters and is thus exposed to a host of possible points and paths of interception. Although the Electronic Communications Privacy Act of 1986 specifically forbids eavesdropping on electronic transmissions, laws of that kind are extraordinarily difficult to enforce because no policing agency controls the points of access. This basic lack of control is a major impediment to the growth of electronic commerce.

The need to guarantee information integrity presents a second security problem. Once information is put on-line, its creators can do little to ensure that it will not be altered electronically. Thus hospitals worry about patients' records being changed, and authors and publishers are concerned that their views might be misrepresented. Moreover, just as the nature of the Internet makes it difficult to detect the theft of information, its current structure also makes it virtually impossible to trace tampering. Anyone can operate on-line under a false name. A *New Yorker* cartoon makes the point: A dog, sitting at a computer keyboard, turns to his canine companion and remarks, "On the Internet, nobody knows you're a dog." As the Internet grows, security problems are likely to mount. In 1990, the federally funded Computer Emergency Response Team reported 130 break-ins on the Internet. According to an article in *Technology Review*, that number grew to 1,300 in 1993 and 2,300 in 1994.

Usually break-ins, like tampering, fraud, and theft, are considered to be within the purview of governmental agencies. But on the Internet, governments have not yet defined precisely what constitutes theft, nor have they established the institutions to trace or apprehend thieves. So the field is wide open to private development. The most obvious opportunity lies with the technologies of electronic security. Theoretically, cutting-edge technologies such as encryption and fire walls can solve security problems by fully protecting on-line transmissions. (Fire walls protect a company's internal network from outside users by establishing physical filters between networks.) Neither technology has been perfected or widely deployed, but many industry insiders believe that within a year or two, both will be powerful enough to guarantee the security of transactions. And the companies that reach perfection first will generate a new current of enthusiasm for commercial activity on the Net. At the moment, the leader in digital-security software is RSA Data Security, which has already licensed its encryption algorithms to major Net players such as IBM and Netscape. Other companies, such as Verisign and Microsoft, have also joined the race.

Meanwhile, there is another race going on, a race less obvious in some respects but ultimately more important. The development of secure technologies is absolutely critical to the expansion of Internet commerce, but it is not sufficient. To facilitate the expansion of electronic commerce, even the most sophisticated technologies will have to be embedded in broader, more secure networks. And those networks, along with their security systems, will have to be managed by some trusted intermediary. Enter again private companies, making rules and managing virtual communities.

To facilitate the expansion of electronic commerce, even the most sophisticated technologies will have to be embedded in broader, more secure networks.

On-line communities are necessary because individual security precautions have only a limited value on the Net. Value lies, instead, in a wider, protected community of users, who can communicate among themselves confidentially and thus confidently. The value of the community is created by the entities that run and manage it. They are the ones who determine its size, choose its members, implement security provisions, and punish violators. If the Internet is a lawless frontier, then these service providers are the new marshals in town. Unlike the old marshals, though, they are also constructing the towns and then marketing them by bragging about the local security and clientele. Wyatt Earp would have drooled.

Communities and commerce

For on-line communities to form, content providers need to feel confident about whom they are dealing with, how their material is being used, and how they are receiving payment. What they need, in short, is an entity to transform the anonymity and anarchy of the Internet into a market with identifiable customers and recordable transactions. That entity would manage a corner of the Internet where explicit rules and norms would prevail.

Early forms of management entities already exist in such Internet service providers as UUnet, PSINet, and Bolt Beranek & Newman. But the services they make available are still minimal, limited largely to granting their users a means of access to the Internet and some tools for navigating it. What these providers could offer (and presumably soon will) are the value-added services associated with rules and rule making. They could, for instance, provide secure transaction services, limit access to certain groups, or cluster their users into communities linked by similar interests or needs.

Such communities already exist on-line in the form of chat groups and bulletin boards. But their rapid proliferation has undermined some of the Net's early sense of community and begun to raise concerns among some users about the risks of association with unknown, untraceable parties. Some users, especially old-time hackers and technophiles, will probably want to remain in the vast, anonymous realm of the open Web. But others—parents who want their children reading the *Encyclopaedia Britannica* but not *Hustler*, researchers who tire of their professional discussions being interrupted by outsiders, technophobic shoppers who love L.L. Bean but hate keyboards—will probably prefer to exchange the adventure of cyberspace for a more regulated and predictable community. Service providers can fill this need by creating customized, managed communities in cyberspace and setting their own standards for on-line exchange.

To set and maintain those standards, service providers will need to employ many of the technologies described earlier. They will need, for example, an accurate means of tracking who is on-line and what those people are doing. That way, any content provider can learn who is making use of its product and, more important, can be paid for its "microsales" to those users. Armed with the appropriate tracking and billing technologies, the service provider would perform the crucial functions of intermediation: It would track customers, bill them, and pay content providers. It would also guarantee that violators of the rules would be punished, most likely by expulsion from the community.

Microsoft Network is one example of this trend toward on-line communities. Originally conceived as another proprietary on-line service, MSN has recently been repositioned as an Internet community with well-ordered rules and value-added services. Other on-line services, such as AOL, Prodigy, and CompuServe, are similarly reinventing themselves as full-service Internet communities. And they are not alone. Time Warner's popular Pathfinder site—which offers rich content from across the media giant's empire—requires users to register, tracks their subsequent usage, and plans soon to offer accompanying transaction services. Several other telecommunication and media companies have also announced plans to launch their own communities on the Internet.

While the shift toward communities of commerce is most evident in consumer-oriented services, the logic of communities extends even further than that. A computer manufacturer could easily create an Internet community with its key distributors, just as a large clothing company might reap the benefits of establishing a secure transaction infrastructure with its suppliers. Universities could choose to distribute their course catalogs only within their own corners of the Internet, and banks could dedicate separate, secure lines for their own internal transactions. The recent interest in using the Internet as an intracompany business tool—an "Intranet"—is yet another variation on those themes.

Service providers and an improved Internet

In all these examples, the companies managing the on-line transactions of their users would have created privately ruled communities, just as developers in some urban areas have built private "towns," complete with strict rules, security forces, and gates to keep outsiders away. To build these communities, service providers would employ encryption, fire walls, and other evolving technologies to control access in the same way as developers control it in physical communities.

This vision—of walls and guards and tracked activities—is precisely opposed to the open market and universal access approved of by most Internet proponents. It is also seemingly at odds with the democracy that mass electronic communication is thought to foster. But although private towns may well undermine the broad goals of an open, egalitarian society, managed virtual communities do not restrict the prospects for free, open communication. They merely divide the realms of activity, just as most people already divide their own activities into private and public spheres. Moreover, by establishing limited, ordered communities, service providers have the potential to increase dramatically the number of people who venture on-line. For despite the terrific growth in Internet use, many people still find cyberspace too noisy, too anarchic, and too cumbersome for their purposes. By restricting the on-line options, fine-tuning the offerings to match a select group of users, and offering some means of recourse in case of fraud or abuse, service providers can develop the kinds of managed communities that will draw new users on-line and increase the productivity of those already there.

[Internet] service providers can . . . create a commercial space that would bring together buyers, sellers, browsers, and advertisers in a regulated, orderly community.

Most important, though, service providers can create an environment conducive to commerce. As long as the Internet remains an open, unregulated space, companies from information-intensive industries such as publishing, software, and financial services are unlikely to shift large segments of their business on-line. They may advertise or encourage chat groups to discuss their products, but they probably will not sell them directly through cyberspace. To make the final leap, they—and presumably all content providers—need systems of property rights and exchange, as well as a means of enforcement. Central governments are not now in a position to make or enforce the needed rules, and the Internet as a whole has no controlling body. Individual companies or entrepreneurs are likely to develop the technological means for implementing rules—encryption, fire walls, tracking systems, and so on—but only if they have some prospect of reaping the benefits from their investment or innovation. Service providers can facilitate the development of a market by purchasing or licensing the technologies from their creators and then using them to create a commercial space that would bring together buyers, sellers, browsers, and advertisers in a regulated, orderly community.

In the long run, the Internet will not transform business into a friction-free realm in which millions of anonymous buyers and sellers meet for one-shot, instantaneous transactions. Nor will the Net remain unregulated and uncensored. Portions of the Net may stay that way, but they will not be busy with commerce. Rather, commerce will migrate to areas where rules prevail and responsibility can be assigned. Some of those areas probably will appear unorganized, and transactions within them will take place faster and more cheaply than in the physical world. But increased speed and reduced costs will not lead to the disappearance of rules, communities, or intermediaries. On the contrary, the real move to electronic commerce will demand several layers of intermediaries to form new communities and support new rules. Electronic commerce requires those changes, which will also provide companies with the greatest opportunity for profit. In cyberspace, the real power will lie with those who make the rules.

Notes

1. The argument of this section draws extensively on the work and writings of Douglass C. North. See, in particular, North, *Structure and Change in Economic History* (New York: W.W. Norton & Company, 1981); and North and Robert P. Thomas, *The Rise of the Western World: A New Economic History* (Cambridge: Cambridge University Press, 1973).

5

Internet Technology Will Be Embedded in Everyday Products

David Kline

David Kline is a contributing writer for the monthly magazine Wired, *a commentator for National Public Radio, and coauthor of* Road Warriors: Dreams and Nightmares Along the Information Highway.

Embedded systems—tiny computers that are embedded within everyday products—could have as much of an impact on social and economic life as the electric motor did in the early 1900s. The Internet could expand beyond PCs to invisibly link automobiles, telephones, televisions, CD players, and many other products whose functions would be controlled by a microprocessor, operating system, and software. Smaller memory requirements would enable these embedded products to become very affordable for hundreds of millions of consumers.

If you want to glimpse the future of the Internet (and of computing itself), look to the history of the electric motor.

A hundred years ago, electric motors were relatively large "stand-alone" devices. They had to be constructed from machined parts, or else purchased and installed by trained mechanics. By all accounts, more than a little skill was required to operate these devices.

Over the course of several decades, however, the design and operation of electric motors became more standardized, their power requirements and internal mechanisms miniaturized, and their manufacture and sale commoditized. By 1918, the Sears, Roebuck and Co. catalog offered a 5-pound Home Motor, suitable for a variety of applications, for only US$8.75—equivalent to about $85 today.

"The many attachments shown on this page," the catalog advertisement promised, "may be operated by this motor and help to lighten the burden of the home." And, indeed, surrounding the ad for the Home Motor were companion ads for what might loosely be called "plug-ins" or

David Kline, "The Embedded Internet," *Wired*, October 1996. Copyright © Wired Magazine Group, Inc. All rights reserved. Reprinted by permission.

"helper applications." There was a Beater Attachment ("whips cream and beats eggs when used in connection with the Home Motor"), a Fan Attachment ("includes fan and guard, which can be quickly attached to Home Motor"), a Churn and Mixer Attachment ("for which you will find many uses"), Buffer and Grinder Attachments ("will be found very useful in many ways around the home"), and, last but not least, a Vibrator Attachment ("includes three applicators and handle"). To what uses the Vibrator Attachment was put was not explained—and readers will probably find their still-living grandmothers or great-grandmothers somewhat less than forthcoming on the subject.

From electric motors to embedded systems

In those days, the new Home Motor was the subject of excited discussion in cafés and businesses and around the dinner table, much as home PCs and the Internet are today. It's easy to imagine industrial-age early adopters evangelizing their friends and relatives about the benefits of home motor technology ("You can beat 20 eggs in the time it takes you to do 2 by hand"). Likewise, one can picture curmudgeons of the day rolling their eyes at all those frothy Motorheads ("Pardon me, but who needs 20 eggs?"), just as comedians poke fun at Netheads today.

> *In [a universal Internet], the common artifacts of daily life . . . are all connected via cheap automated software in a global network [known as] the "embedded Internet."*

Today, of course, the Home Motor is no longer a cultural icon. Indeed, electric motor technology has become literally invisible, embedded inside thousands of everyday products, from hair dryers and pencil sharpeners to dishwashers and toys. Hardly obsolete, the Home Motor is instead a victim of its own success, ignored precisely because of its ubiquity. It has become a central—albeit invisible—fact of daily life.

Can it be that, as the electric motor goes, so goes the Internet? More to the point: what will it take for the Net to become so embedded in social and economic life—so central to everyday communication and commerce—that it becomes as invisible and ubiquitous a feature of daily life as the electric motor?

We may have the answer to that question sooner than we think. A little-known technology—far more significant than Java—is about to be deployed on the Internet. This technology could rapidly transform the Net into a medium with genuine mass-market penetration in our society. It will not only greatly expand the Net's role as a mass consumer medium, but will also change it into a powerful industrial force that will reshape the dynamics of the market and the competitive strategies of businesses by the end of the 1990s.

What is this miracle technology? It's called "embedded systems"— tiny crash-proof computers that are embedded or hardwired within everyday products and dedicated to the performance of specific tasks or groups of tasks. Already used in a host of industrial and consumer products, from antilock brakes to VCRs to microwaves, embedded systems typically offer significantly faster, much cheaper, and far more reliable real-time performance than the cumbersome multipurpose or "fat" software used in PCs. In fact, already 90 percent of the world's microprocessors are used not in PCs, but are hidden inside common household or electronics products.

Now, thanks to new technical advances made by embedded systems developers, these invisible computers have become Internet-ready. Embedded software now offers automated Net connectivity with about 1/100th the memory required by Windows and other PC operating systems, at about 1/10th the cost.

For David St. Charles, president and CEO of $100 million Integrated Systems Inc. (ISI), the market leader among embedded systems developers, this sort of cheap Net connectivity opens up enormous new possibilities. Indeed, he offers a vision of a truly universal Internet. In it, the common artifacts of daily life—a car, a TV, a CD player, a phone, a piece of office equipment, a natural gas meter, a PC—are all connected via cheap automated software in a global network he calls the "embedded Internet."

"This is the next stage," St. Charles says in his measured, Canadian voice. "This is where we make the Internet real. And I mean, as ubiquitous as electric motors or telephones, where all sorts of devices and systems are linked invisibly together. Where people and devices easily and automatically communicate with each other with no one having to know anything about computers or software or TCP/IP [Transmission Control Protocol/Internet Protocol] stacks or anything else. It's everywhere, it does everything, and it's absolutely a no-brainer to use. The push-button Internet!"

Here, at last, is a vision of the Internet for the masses, in their hundreds of millions and ultimately in their billions. In it, the Net is no longer just a publishing or an entertainment or a personal communications medium, but rather a fundamental and indispensable engine driving all social and economic life. It's an industrial medium that enables automated monitoring and reporting on factory-floor production; a home security and emergency response medium far more reliable than today's phone-based 911 system; a medical medium through which patient treatment plans are automatically routed to relevant providers; a consumer appliance and office equipment medium that checks the status of devices and initiates electronic repairs; a utility management medium in which power usage is read and managed remotely. You name the application, the Net will be essential to it.

Here, at last, is an Internet finally set free from its PC-centric straitjacket—a cyberspace transformed from just another platform into an omnipresent glue that binds the whole of society, with all its trillions of daily social and economic interactions, into a truly connected civilization.

But the secret to all this, insists St. Charles, is invisibility. "If you want the Internet to be everywhere," he says, "it has to be visible nowhere. It has to be unseen, unnoticed, undiscussed."

Disappearing act

To be sure, "unseen" is not a word we would normally use to describe either the Net or the computing devices we use to access it. As Interval Research Corp.'s Brenda Laurel so adroitly puts it, using computers is like going to the movie theater and having to watch the projector instead of the movie.

In similar fashion, St. Charles regards the current iconization of the Internet in media and cultural circles as a sign not of its assimilation into American social and economic life, but of how far it still must go to become a medium of commerce and communications for the masses. In his view, we'll know that the Net has truly arrived when there are no more Internet cafés, no more Internet seminars, and no more Internet magazines (or, for that matter, articles such as the one you're reading now).

This makes sense when you look at technologies that have achieved genuine mass-market penetration in our society. After all, you don't see any magazines called *Dial Tone Today* that feature the latest ins and outs of the Net's closest cousin, telephony. In fact, we hardly even see the telephone anymore—we simply use it, thinking only of what we want to do with it. The technology, in direct proportion to its becoming a central fact of daily existence, has become invisible.

"Invisibility, you might say, is my business," says St. Charles. "It's what I do for a living—I make technology disappear."

Embedded systems . . . can be optimized to deliver a [superior] level of speed, reliability, and low cost.

He's not kidding, either. Once called "the Microsoft of hidden computers" by *Forbes* magazine, ISI's technology appears to be everywhere. It is embedded inside Sony direct broadcast satellites, Motorola communications satellites, Kodak and Xerox printers and copiers, Hewlett-Packard interactive TV set-top boxes, Sega karaoke systems, Gilbarco automated gas pumps, Boeing airliners, Avis rental-car navigation systems, Philips consumer appliances, as well as AT&T, Northern Telecom, and Alcatel switching equipment, to name a few.

"Most people have no idea what our industry does or how deeply our work affects their lives," St. Charles notes, "despite the fact that in many ways it has probably done more than Microsoft and the whole PC industry to bring computing technology into people's day-to-day lives. If you ask people how many computers they use, they'll probably say one—their desktop PC. But the reality is, it's probably more like 15. They use computers to drive the tape in their VCRs, and they use them in their microwaves, cars, automatic teller machines, gas pumps, phone systems—you name it, these days it's probably got an embedded computer in it."

So what exactly is an embedded computer? Very simply, an embedded computer is a microprocessor, a real-time operating system and application software that has been built into a larger product to handle the control functions of that product. Typically, an embedded systems company such as ISI delivers just the master software—the real-time operating system and application code—to the end-product manufacturer, which buys and installs the microprocessors and other hardware components.

The advantage of embedded systems is that, partly because they are dedicated to the performance of a single task or specific group of tasks, they can be optimized to deliver a level of speed, reliability, and low cost that PC hardware and software manufacturers could never in their wildest dreams hope to achieve. And as for ease of use—let's just say that the PC industry is not even on the same planet as the masses of ordinary consumers.

Only in the PC industry is it considered customary to sell products so unreliable and confusing that nearly a third of buyers are unable to use them without help. According to Dataquest, some 200 million calls to PC technical-support hotlines were made by users in 1996. And of those calls made during peak midday hours, only one in seven will even get past a busy signal. In contrast, when was the last time you had to "install" your TV, your phone, or your VCR? And when was the last time you had to call technical support because your microwave wouldn't work or you couldn't figure out how to use it?

Truth be told, the PC is radically different in design from any other technology or appliance used by the general consuming public. Indeed, if Intel and Microsoft had designed our kitchens, we'd probably all be using $3,000 multipurpose "Kitchen Processors" rather than the low-cost, dedicated, push-button appliances we now have. These Kitchen Processors, of course, would need to be configured and launched to, say, heat coils for a toasting application, and then reconfigured and relaunched to heat incandescent filament for a lighting application.

As the basis for a truly ubiquitous Internet, today's PC simply won't cut it. But will the embedded Internet approach be realized only in the far-distant future? Apparently not, for Integrated Systems has already built Java and HTML [HyperText Markup Language] capability into its open embedded operating system, known as pSOS. And the company has already signed a deal with Philips for an under-$300 Net-communicating browser appliance. It is also in talks with a number of other telecom, industrial, and consumer electronics firms to embed Net-ready computer systems into everyday consumer products, from smart kitchen appliances that communicate among themselves to automated automobile diagnostic systems that flag mechanics about needed repairs.

And ISI is not the only company bringing its hidden computer expertise to the world of the Net. Iowa-based Microware Systems Corporation has also announced an embedded Internet strategy and is working with Mitsubishi on a TV with Web capability integrated into its circuitry. This Web TV enables VGA [Video Graphics Array]-quality graphics, something that cannot be done via a Web box atop the TV, and it will cost only $200 more to produce than regular TV models. Microware has also signed with Uniden to produce an Internet-capable phone that collects email, and with Hongkong Telecom IMS to deliver a Java-enabled version of DAVID, a highly regarded digital TV platform, to provide online services over television to homes in Hong Kong.

The industrial net

Even more significant than the consumer uses of embedded Internet technology may be its industrial potential. Indeed, embedded systems that use the Net to reduce industrial costs and streamline commercial operations—the "Industrial Net," if you will—are likely to deliver far more in the way of real bankable revenues in the next few years than will consumer applications.

ISI, for example, is working with Xionics and other office equipment firms to embed low-cost Net capability into millions of printers and other office peripherals. These firms hope to achieve multimillion-dollar savings in labor and service costs by performing remote equipment diagnostics and maintenance via the Net.

How would each printer get connected to the Net? It could be through phone lines, electrical wiring, a LAN [local area network], or even a "spread-spectrum" system using low-power radio signals to feed the data to a wired or wireless gateway.

And why use the Net rather than simple phone lines? Only the Internet can serve as the infrastructure for a truly connected world. As a medium, it is much cheaper than the phone network. It provides standardized interoperability between all types of disparate devices, networks, and systems. The Net is also a better platform than the phone system for adding intelligence and agent technology. And the Net's distributed architecture makes it more efficient at rerouting communications around damage and bottlenecks.

A truly Net-connected world requires that the medium be woven into the basic infrastructure of society, including our public services.

But perhaps most importantly, the Net's packet-switched approach to handling communications is simply better suited to handling the billions—or even trillions—of relatively short data transmissions likely in a future connected world than is the phone network, where each connection essentially requires a dedicated link for the entire duration of the transmission.

One can easily imagine a host of other industrial possibilities. Remote meter reading over the Net by power utilities? Net-communicating smart sensors to remotely manage factory production processes? Low-cost Net-connected alarm systems for the fast-growing home security industry? The potential of embedded Internet technology for industrial uses is enormous.

But beyond its many industrial and consumer applications, a truly Net-connected world requires that the medium be woven into the basic infrastructure of society, including our public services.

"Think about 911," suggests Microware's founder and CEO, Ken Kaplan. "Everyone has access to it, and it's pretty much basic to societal functioning, right? Well, I can foresee a really cheap 911 device that costs just a few dollars and has only one button on it—an embedded Internet pagerlike gadget with a GPS (Global Positioning System) chip and a wireless connection to the Net. You get mugged or have a heart attack—just push the button and help is on the way. It could even be self-actuating if you use a smart sensor to monitor heart activity. The technology already exists for it. All we need is cheap connectivity through a ubiquitous, low-cost, public switched-network that can be automated and doesn't require voice or other human intervention—in other words, the Net."

"You know, maybe I shouldn't have mentioned this idea of a 911 device," worries Kaplan. "I mean, this could be *the* killer app of the embedded Internet, and here I've gone and given it away."

He needn't worry about competition, at least from the ranks of PC hardware and software vendors. To build a 911 device linked to a universal Internet will require design characteristics and product features that are simply not intrinsic to the PC industry. Chief among these are low cost, fast performance, utter simplicity of use, and total crash-proof reliability.

Unlike multipurpose PC operating systems such as Windows, which must take into account every conceivable user input and be able to support a huge variety of applications, an embedded system typically must support only a narrow suite of functions and needs to respond to only a very limited range of human input—like a foot depressing a car brake pedal to activate a computer-controlled antilock braking mechanism. As a result, embedded systems have far smaller memory requirements. For example, ISI's Internet-ready version of its pSOS operating system uses 16 Kbytes of memory, or about 1/100th the memory used by Windows 95.

This enables embedded systems to offer a far more economical approach to building cheap, Net-browsing appliances than those touted by traditional PC industry vendors, such as Oracle with its stripped-down network computer. A full embedded system—hardware and software—that uses Microware's OS-9 operating system costs only about $150. That includes a Net-ready operating system (at $10 a pop), a 32-bit PowerPC processor, and all the components needed for video, input and output ports, a graphical user interface, and a browser. Not bad.

For products not requiring a user interface or input-output extensions, the cost can be even less. An Internet-ready system embedded in your gas meter that enables the power company to conduct remote meter-reading could cost just a few dollars, as presumably would Kaplan's 911 device.

Faster operating systems

The superior performance of embedded systems also derives from the fact that their operating systems are *real-time* operating systems—meaning that Microware's OS-9 and ISI's pSOS react in a rapid and consistent way to events that occur outside the computer, with little if any delay imposed by the computer itself. This is partly due to the entirely different design methodology that embedded computer companies have adopted to sell their systems to companies that use them in mission-critical applications.

Consider, for example, that when a PC user types a keyboard command and the system hangs for a moment, it's at most an annoyance. But when a driver speeding along a rain-slicked freeway at 65 mph slams his foot on the brakes and a wheel locks up, any delay by the computer in modulating the brakes can be a fatality.

"Bugs?" says Microware's Kaplan. "For us they're a disaster. For PC software companies, they're an additional revenue opportunity." Meaning, of course, that this year's software bug is next year's purchasable upgrade.

Indeed, Kaplan argues, few people realize how different embedded software design is from the approach used in the desktop PC industry. "In the PC world, software design is an iterative process. Back and forth it goes, from the programmers to the internal test group and then back to the code writers, until it's more or less ready to test on beta users. Microsoft sent its prerelease Windows 95 OS [operating system] out to about half a million beta testers. Those people managed to catch some of the bugs, but as we all know, not all. Well, there's no way in hell that we can send beta software to Boeing and then wait for planes to start falling from the sky to discover the bugs."

According to Kaplan, each stage of the embedded systems design process has specification and quality objectives that absolutely must be met before the code moves on to the next stage—an approach more typical of aerospace firms than PC companies.

Embedded systems are the only way to make the Internet as cheap, easy, and transparent as the electric motor or the phone.

Translate those very different design methodologies of the PC and embedded systems industries to the world of Net-enabled 911 devices imagined by Kaplan. Would you trust your life to an emergency-response device built by a PC vendor, even assuming the device could be built at a consumer price point? There does not seem to be much point in having a 911 device if it's going to crash from time to time.

The need for mission-critical design is not limited just to applications where lives are at stake, notes Kaplan. "Even in the world of everyday consumer electronics, customers simply will not put up with the glitches and breakdowns and user confusion common to PCs. Anyone who wants to bring the Net to the masses had better understand that."

Furthermore, when we imagine Net-enabled applications used by hundreds of millions of people, there must be a degree of social assurance—much like the certainty of hearing a dial tone when we pick up the phone—that somehow, in the background somewhere, the whole underlying system is doing its job and performing as promised.

Ordinary people are the key

The invisible Internet does not mean the end of PCs—indeed, the ranks of today's full-featured PC users will continue to grow. Nor does it mean that Net capabilities must be dumbed down to only those applications and uses possible in a simple push-button device. The concept of the embedded Internet simply recognizes that epochal technological change generally comes to the world on the world's terms, shaped by human nature and our existing political economy. To be sure, slowly and imperceptibly at first, new technologies also reshape us. But the starting point for tomorrow's great technology-induced social changes must be the masses of technologically unsophisticated ordinary consumers.

"These are the people who need to become wired if the Net is really to grow into the enormous social and economic force it is capable of becoming," insists Kaplan. "You say the Net will change the world? Well, those people are the world. So you had better design a Net-connected world that ordinary people can really understand and use."

In other words, instead of trying to get everyone to go out and buy a PC and try to master its arcane methodology, simply put Net connectivity inside the everyday devices and systems that people already use. Bring the mountain to Muhammad, as it were.

Adds ISI's St. Charles: "Embedded systems are the only way to make the Internet as cheap, easy, and transparent as the electric motor or the phone. It's the only way to make the Net a basic and ubiquitous fact of life. It's that simple."

6

Competition, Rules, and Technology Can Increase Access to the Internet

Reed Hundt

Reed Hundt is the chairman of the Federal Communications Commission (FCC), a federal agency that regulates American radio, television, satellite, and cable communications.

The rapid growth of Internet users and services has created the need to maximize bandwidth (the capacity and speed of networks) and access to cyberspace. To achieve this objective, competition must be encouraged among Internet service providers in order to reduce access costs and attract more users. Policies and standards should be created to facilitate access to the Internet. And technological innovations such as an all-digital telephone network would expand bandwidth and ease Internet congestion.

Editor's note: The following speech was delivered at the INET '96 conference in Montreal, Canada, on June 28, 1996.

Here we are at last, smack dab in the digital age; an age of promise, an age of possibility; and for many an age of anxiety, apprehension, and alarm.

The embodiment of this era is, in all respects, the Internet. This is a technology every bit as revolutionary as the invention of the telegraph was over 150 years ago.

The Internet grew out of a small project started by the U.S. Department of Defense to link up four military research centers. Similarly, the telegraph got its start as a small government grant—$30,000 awarded in 1843 led Samuel Morse to the first test of a telegraph line from Washington, D.C. to Baltimore in 1844.

The Internet can help us achieve many goals we've had since that first city-to-city click. Even though it's been 150 years since Samuel Morse's invention, much of the world does not yet have basic telephone service,

Reed Hundt, "Access + Bandwidth = Communications Revolution," a speech delivered at the INET '96 Conference, Montreal, Canada, June 28, 1996.

millions of American households do not have active phone service, and our kids spend each day in classrooms, 90% of which are unconnected to the world of information.

The growth of the Internet provides new ways to bring all children and all Americans into the information age. Today I want to talk about the questions we face in assuring that we can realize the full promise of the Internet.

In preparing for this speech, I asked my staff to explain to me how the Internet works. They said I wouldn't understand. I told them I was the first FCC Chairman to have a computer on my desk. That's our point, they said.

I persisted—so in desperation they resorted to charts. Then they showed me a picture of a plate of spaghetti. The Internet, they said, looks like this. And they showed me pictures of trains in a switch yard. It works like that, they said. Then they showed me curves that sloped up like the ascent of Everest. It's growing like that, they said.

Then they told me that, based on current projections, in the year 2010 there will be more Internet users than people on the planet. That's a little hard to get your mind around. But I imagine that at least by then *Slate* [a Microsoft publication on the World Wide Web] will be making money.

Here's what I took away from these desperate, nearly hopeless efforts to explain the Internet to a lawyer. The Internet changes everything. Its digital code turns a zero into a window on infinity and a one into a unifier of economies and society. It turns the world upside down. In the words of Jimi Hendrix, a six becomes nine, and I don't mind.

Jimi Hendrix is, I know, a historical figure who needs explanation for the Internet group. He is a person whose accomplishments in the musical field are memorialized in a Seattle museum owned by Paul Allen, cofounder of Traf-O-Data, a small Seattle business that changed its name some years ago to, if I remember correctly, Microsoft.

And because the Internet changes everything about the way we communicate, it necessarily changes all our governmental communications policies. To drill down a little deeper: it would be more accurate to say that the Internet gives us the opportunity to change all our communications policies.

George Washington Plunkett, the famous nineteenth-century politico in New York explained the secret of his success this way: "I seen my opportunities and I took them." So what should we do with the opportunity to change communications policy that the Internet gives us?

Five important questions

I see five major questions that need answering at the get-go:

1. How can public policy promote or at least not deter expansion of bandwidth to power up the development of the Internet?
2. What rules can we get rid of and what rules should we write to promote the development of the Internet?
3. Should we be concerned that the economics of pricing on the Internet—influenced as they are by current out-of-date regulatory policies—won't in fact sustain development of the Internet?

4. How can we make sure that Internet reaches all Americans, especially kids in classrooms?

5. How can we make sure the Internet reaches across the globe? Don't we need government policy in the United States and worldwide to guarantee that Internet access becomes a truly universal product? Don't we need to guarantee that everyone gets access to the common network of networks?

We at the FCC have seen the benefits of the Internet firsthand.

One of my first actions as Chairman of the FCC was to speed the replacement of the outdated FCC communications equipment and mainframe computer systems with a state of the art internal computer network, ISDN [Integrated Service Digital Network] phones, and PCs on all staff desktops. In 1995 I unplugged our 25-year-old mainframe because we can now do much more with networked PCs and workstations than we ever could with that behemoth in the basement.

Based on current projections, in the year 2010 there will be more Internet users than people on the planet.

If anyone is looking for a good deal on a used Honeywell, come talk to me after the speech. I'll even throw in a bunch of rotary phones that we still have lying around.

When we put up our World Wide Web site in 1994, we initially got about 100 hits a day. That reflected our low-budget operation and the small community of lobbyists who normally visit us. But our goal was to open up our doors on the Net and let all Americans participate. We're getting there. We now get 50,000 hits a day and transfer almost 400 megabytes of data. We get visits from more than 50,000 unique hosts every month.

To some of you, this may not sound like a big deal, since there are now many sites that get over a million hits a day. But, for the first time, members of the public can get copies of FCC information shortly after it's released—or months later—and for no charge. We couldn't afford to duplicate and mail copies of our decisions and resource materials to every home, or even every public library in America. But we can put everything online, where anyone in the world with an Internet connection can get access to it.

The explosion of external communication with the FCC is nothing compared to what has happened inside our walls, up and down our linoleum-lined halls. Not only are we on the Net—we are accommodating our own internal communications and networking needs via an intranet and remote access connections to our servers.

What this shows is that an open, distributed, interoperable packet-switched network is an incredibly powerful force for change.

The success and openness of the Internet is attracting a proliferation of new services. Streaming video and audio may alter TV and radio as we know them in the long run. But in the short run, these and other new services give us three major objectives—bandwidth and access, more bandwidth and more access, and even more bandwidth and even more access.

That's what our policies should promote, facilitate, encourage, or at least avoid deterring.

The traditional communications industries don't think in this way. They think they are in the telephone business, or the broadcast business, or the satellite business. They don't think they are in the access and bandwidth business—but they are. And when people used to think of the FCC, they thought about universal service, affordable rates, and quality service. Now they recognize, I hope, that we're in the access and bandwidth business.

Or, to be honest, when people think about the FCC, they think about radio shock jock Howard Stern. But all these issues—yes, even Howard—are really about bandwidth.

Our policies have too long and too often been focussed on services: how to keep local telephone prices or cable rates low, or how to get lower accounting rates on international telephone calls.

Bandwidth and access are not goals that presuppose any particular service. They are means not ends, and over time our focus on services can diminish even as our zeal to maximize bandwidth and access is unabated. After all, if the bandwidth and access are there, the services will be invented. Indeed, visions of services are dancing through the heads of you in this room. Bandwidth on networks accessible to all will make those visions possible.

Building a network

Of course, no one can afford to build, on their own, the spaghetti plate of networks that is not only the Internet but also the underlying telephone network. Government is necessarily involved in the promotion and development of bandwidth and access.

As Abraham Lincoln said, "The legitimate object of government, is to do for a community of people, whatever they need to have done, but can not do, at all, or can not, so well do, for themselves in their separate and individual capacities."

Building a network to some people—like the FCC's intranet—is something that some communities can do for themselves. Building a network to all people—which is what the Internet should be—is something that needs to be done, but that none of us can do acting alone or so well as if we act through government.

I want to dispel the myth that bandwidth is infinite and access to everyone is guaranteed without collective action. The FCC, like similar agencies in other countries, was created because there are limits on the availability of bandwidth. Over-the-air transmission requires spectrum, of course. Spectrum is bandwidth. By definition spectrum is a scarce resource. If it weren't, we wouldn't have collected $20 billion in spectrum auctions. People don't pay that kind of money for a non-scarce commodity. Spectrum is infinitely inexhaustible, but it is finitely available. You can't use spectrum up by using it, but you can't make more of it than God gave us.

Of course Manhattan is a small island but tall buildings permit more people to use it. Similarly, new [transmission signal] compression techniques make more use of bandwidth than previously thought possible. I just read that a single swatch of six megahertz for digital television need not be limited to a single channel of high resolution picture but can be used for 24 channels of standard definition. That means that the 10 licenses that Congress ordered us to give to the broadcasters of Washington, D.C. can be used for 240 terrestrial over-the-air digital channels. That trumps the satellite industry and even cable. It is a tremendous force for competition.

Our mission is to give consumers and businesses more services, more choices, and more control over those choices—in other words, more bandwidth.

Compression doesn't prove that spectrum is no longer scarce. Even George Gilder [author of *Life After Television*] would agree with that (except possibly in the Keynesian [after English economist John Maynard Keynes] long run—defined as when we're all dead). But compression does prove that market forces, if unleashed, will make more of spectrum than any government policy is likely to do. That's why the idea that digital broadcast licenses should be regulated to produce just one high definition channel may not be a crime, but, in the words of the French diplomat Charles-Maurice de Talleyrand, "it is worse than a crime, it is a blunder."

Bandwidth over wired networks is also a scarce resource, because it costs money to build those wires. We have historically allowed companies to monopolize bandwidth in one region in exchange for the authority to regulate the way those companies offer their services.

In 1984, we opened up the right to offer national bandwidth connections—long distance service—to competition.

In the Telecommunications Act of 1996, Congress gave the FCC a mandate to take the next step and open up local telecommunications markets to real competition. Our mission is to give consumers and businesses more services, more choices, and more control over those choices—in other words, more bandwidth.

Congress also asked the FCC to guarantee universal service, especially to kids in classrooms—in other words, more access.

The future of the Internet, and the ability of [Internet] service providers [ISPs] to offer more bandwidth to their end users, will thus depend on how successful we are at promoting competition in local telecommunications markets and truly universal service.

The right rules

This gets to our second goal: rulewriting or rule-unwriting. We need to write rules that open up the local exchange market. We need to unwrite written rules and undo unwritten rules that inhibit competition.

In August 1996, the FCC issued interconnection rules. I'm going to get technical now—these should permit the spaghetti strands of competing networks to connect at fair prices and terms to each other. All states will impose fair terms and conditions on Bell companies and AT&T and MCI, among others. These terms will translate our rules into the text of the interconnection arrangements available for all network providers and users.

But while we need to write interconnection rules, there are other rules I'm not convinced that we should write.

The FCC has received a petition from the America's Carriers' Telecommunications Association asking that we restrict the sale of "Internet phone" software, because the providers of that software do not comply with the rules that apply to telecommunications carriers. Similar issues are being discussed in other countries, including Canada. We've just finished getting comments on that petition. We're in the process of reviewing those comments now, but I would just note that the National Telecommunications and Information Administration, the Administration's telecommunications expert, has filed very thoughtful and well-reasoned comments with us asking us to reject this petition.

I am also strongly inclined to believe that the right answer at this time is not to place restrictions on software providers, or to subject Internet telephony to the same rules that apply to conventional circuit-switched voice carriers. On the Internet, voice traffic is just a particular kind of data, and imposing traditional regulatory divisions on that data is both counterproductive and futile. Even if most of the FCC wasn't working around the clock on implementation of the Telecommunications Act, I can't imagine that we would have the time to keep track of all the bits passing over the Internet to separate the "acceptable" data packets from the "unacceptable" voice packets.

> *When we have competition among network providers, many of the pricing problems we now address through regulation will be resolved by competition instead.*

More importantly, we shouldn't be looking for ways to subject new technologies to old rules. Instead, we should be trying to fix the old rules so that if those new technologies really are better, they will flourish in the marketplace. For years, some engineers have been telling us that voice over a packet switched network wasn't possible. The latency periods were too great, they said, and you'd never get acceptable quality. Well, it is going to be possible, and in the short period of time since the first commercial products became available, the quality has been rapidly improving. But the last thing we want to do is stop that improvement by thoughtless regulation.

Internet telephony may well become, in time, a competitive alternative to traditional circuit-switched voice telephony. After all, as the growth of the cellular industry demonstrates, people are willing to give up a significant level of quality in exchange for other benefits. In the cellular case, the benefit is the ability to make a call from virtually anywhere; in the case of Internet telephony, the benefit is a vastly lower price. This is especially true, for example, for international telephone calls.

And now the third goal: an economically sustainable regime. Economics is about the marketplace sending signals that compel users and service providers to do the right thing, to utilize the network in the best and most efficient way, and to encourage the network to be built out in ways that, for example, avoid brownouts by building in redundancy.

When we have competition among network providers, many of the pricing problems we now address through regulation will be resolved by competition instead. Consumers will be able to choose a communications company that gives them the best deal on subscription charges, service availability, and charges for making calls. Although competition is seldom perfect, we look forward to being able to rely on it.

One problem that competition might not resolve, though, is that, under anything like today's network architecture, someone who wants to call me has no choice but to deal with the carrier that I have chosen to provide my connection. There's a monopoly relationship there, however many carriers vie for my choice. The monopolist on terminating calls to my home doesn't charge me but charges those who make the calls, so I may not care very much (or even know) how much it charges. So, as the econo-guys [economists] would say, there's a monopoly problem exacerbated by a principal-agent problem.

Traffic on the Internet

What then is the appropriate economic model that can sustain the Internet?

With the number of users and host computers connected to the Internet roughly doubling each year, and traffic on the Internet increasing at an even greater rate, the potential for congestion is increasing rapidly. The growth of the Internet, and evidence of performance degradation, has led some observers, including Bob Metcalfe, the inventor of Ethernet and founder of 3Com [a San Francisco computer hardware manufacturer], to predict that the network will soon collapse from excessive usage.

Because the Internet interconnects thousands of different networks, each of which only controls the traffic passing over its own portion of the network, there is no centralized mechanism to ensure that usage at one point on the network does not create congestion at another point. Because the Internet is a packet-switched network, additional usage, up to a certain point, only adds additional delay for packets to reach their destination, rather than preventing a transmission circuit from being opened. This delay may not cause difficulties for e-mail, but could be fatal for real-time services such as video conferencing and Internet telephony.

Moreover, at a certain point, Internet routers are simply unable to handle the load and will "drop" packets, causing network "brownouts." Such brownouts are already occurring. A group of high-energy physics researchers recently sent a memo to the Federal Networking Council complaining about "catatonic" connections that made it impossible to effectively share scientific data over the Internet.

It's like [Hall of Fame baseball catcher] Yogi Berra's old line about a popular restaurant: "Nobody ever goes there any more; it's too crowded."

Even if individual providers upgrade their networks to achieve sufficient capacity, end users may still experience congestion delays when their traffic must traverse another backbone provider's network, or the smaller networks to which the receiving computer is connected. Standards bodies are developing new standards to reduce congestion and make possible more reliable connections for bandwidth-intensive applications, but these standards must be widely deployed within the network to have a significant effect.

The increasing levels of Internet use are also beginning to affect the telephone network. Carriers engineered and deployed their switches based on the characteristics of voice traffic, where a conversation lasts an average of three minutes and an average customer attempts about three calls per busy hour. Internet users, however, typically engage in far longer calls than voice users. As a result, Internet usage is placing unexpected demand on local exchange carriers' switches, to the point that switch congestion is threatening service quality for voice users of some switches.

This might not be such a big problem if we had an all-digital phone network that was based on a packet-routing multimedia technology such as ATM. But we don't, yet. We've got hundreds of billions of dollars of plant in the ground that works fine for voice, but that gets strained by the requirements of data communications. So the hard question is: if there are costs for upgrading the network to support the explosion of Internet and other data usage, who pays those costs?

The FCC decided in the early 1980s that enhanced service providers, which include Internet service providers, should not be subject to the interstate access charges that long-distance carriers pay to local phone companies for originating and terminating calls. ISPs are therefore treated as "end users" and can purchase lines that have no per-minute usage-based charge for receiving calls from their customers. The phone companies argue that the absence of usage charges means that ISPs do not provide the revenue to cover the additional costs they impose on the network.

I don't know what the full answer is to this problem. But I'm inclined to believe our best guidance is to let technology, competition, and access reform make the problem go away. We are working to open markets so that these forces can operate most effectively.

As the Internet becomes a part of daily life for more and more people, reliability and service quality will be increasingly essential.

I'm also aware that as the Internet becomes a part of daily life for more and more people, reliability and service quality will be increasingly essential. Whose job is it to minimize the likelihood that the network will go down? In June 1996, Netcom's 400,000 customers lost connectivity to the Internet for more than 13 hours. I don't want to single out Netcom because they aren't the only company that has had this kind of outage, and because this is ultimately an industry-wide issue. How would we feel if Montreal lost its telephone service for a day? I might be happy that no one from my office in Washington could reach me, but I would be concerned about being unable to get in touch with my family.

We have a Network Reliability and Operability Council in the United States that addresses these issues for the telephone network. It reports regularly to the FCC, but it's an industry-led group. I know the Internet has the IETF [Internet Engineering Task Force] which does a very effective job in setting standards. I hope that an appropriate body can be developed for addressing the issues of reliability in the context of the Internet.

The need for universal service

And now the fourth goal: ensuring the availability of bandwidth to all Americans, especially kids in classrooms. We have an obligation—legally, morally, and economically—to promote universal service, especially for those with limited resources. The value of networks increases exponentially as more people are connected. In addition, the Internet rides on top of the existing public switched telephone network, and the rapid growth of the Internet is driven in part by the universal deployment of traditional telephone networks.

Ensuring that schools, libraries, health care providers, and poor, rural, and insular communities benefit from the Internet and the new communications revolution it represents is one of the great challenges of the beginning of the twenty-first century. Government can no longer assume that it can meet public policy objectives by directing regulated or public companies to invest in a certain manner. But the private sector must also contribute its fair share if we are to escape from what the econo-people call the tragedy of the commons.

So today, I challenge the Internet community to provide two years of free Internet access to classrooms and libraries.

On this and other issues we find that the challenge is to find ways to work together—governments, businesses, service providers, researchers, and educational institutions—to solve common problems. Because it's in everyone's interest to have more bandwidth. It's in everyone's interest to have ubiquitous access. And it's in everyone's interest to minimize the artificial barriers placed on the free flow of information.

As the Federal Court in Philadelphia properly recognized in June 1996 in enjoining enforcement of the Communications Decency Act [a law, also known as the Exon Amendment, regulating indecent material on the Internet], the Internet is a new medium. It encompasses some aspects of traditional media such as broadcast and telephony, but it is much more than that. Whether or not it was a wise decision to pass the Exon Amendment—and the Court has said it was not—we still need to recognize that if kids have access to the Internet at home and in classrooms, then parents and teachers need software filters and other tools that empower them to make choices. I've talked to Tim Berners-Lee [cocreator of the World Wide Web] about this, and he said he and his very able team are working on addressing this very problem with the PICS [Platform for Internet Content Selection] system.

If we want, as I do, for our children to ride the information highway from Carthage, Tennessee to the Library of Congress, we can't permit the virtual school bus driver that takes them on that field trip to travel through the red light district. It's legitimate to challenge the Communications Decency Act in court but again, it's not enough to just say no. Your policy goal and our policy goal has got to be to fulfill the promise of the Internet, not just protect the problems of the Internet from governmental solutions.

My final point is that our Internet policies must be international, because the Internet is an inherently global medium.

Although the largest concentration of Internet users is still in the United States, the fastest growth is occurring in other countries. Internet users may not even know where in the world content providers are located. Material that is legal in one country may be illegal elsewhere. It doesn't make sense to subject providers in one country to the laws of a different country simply because, unbeknownst to the provider, someone in the second country downloaded its material from the Internet. To the extent that there are legitimate, agreed-upon governmental objectives—such as privacy and protections against fraud—that may be adversely affected by activities conducted over the Internet, governments should look to international, and wherever possible industry-driven solutions, rather than acting unilaterally.

A second critical area in which we must have global solutions is standards. The Internet has been successful because it is based on open, interoperable standards. In addition to technical standards for the transmission of data across the network, frameworks are needed in areas such as electronic payments, intellectual property, commercial codes governing contractual agreements, security, and privacy.

Frameworks are needed in areas such as electronic payments, intellectual property, commercial codes governing contractual agreements, security, and privacy.

As the Internet grows and becomes more commercialized, however, existing mechanisms may not be sufficient. There are many administrative functions that are essential to the smooth functioning of the Internet, which are handled by a variety of different governmental and nongovernmental bodies. We must consider whether any of these functions can be coordinated in a more efficient way, without losing the flexibility and openness of the existing processes. When I say coordinated, I do not mean government-controlled. Although there are occasions where it is useful for governments to participate in the standards process, the process should be international and driven by the private sector. The efforts of Tony Rutkowski and the Internet Law and Policy Forum on issues such as domain name assignment are an encouraging example of how such a process might work.

So we have many challenges before us. I've outlined what I think are some of the most difficult problems because I think they are also the most important. And all of this is important precisely because of what the Internet means for tens of millions of people today, and what it could mean for hundreds of millions more in the next decade.

This came home to me recently when I traveled to Johannesburg [South Africa] for the meeting of the G-7 [the world's seven largest industrialized nations]. While there, I visited the township of Alexandra. Surrounded by 350,000 people from all over the world, I thought about how many of these people came from terrible war torn areas to this frightening township, a place without clean water, electricity or police or jobs.

But while I was there, I looked up and saw around Alexandra Township the towers of the world's second largest digital mobile communications system. These towers deliver telephone calls. They can also deliver the power and the promise of the Internet. I was proud to be there because in Johannesburg we Americans announced the Mickey Leland initiative to bring the Internet to Africa. If you really believe in the theory of the Internet, in the democratization of this medium, and the need and the ability to reach all people, then you should be the biggest proponents of expanding their access to the Internet. You should support this initiative as well as Net Day [a grassroots effort to link schools' computers to the Internet] and any other effort designed to connect us all.

Bandwidth and access in an information world should be on a par with clean air and water—we are all benefitted when these fundamentals are available from Canada to South Africa; from Alexandria, Virginia to Alexandria, Egypt to Alexandra, South Africa.

7

The National Information Infrastructure Could Be Harmful to Individuals

Alan Wexelblat

Alan Wexelblat is a doctoral student at the Massachusetts Institute of Technology (MIT) Media Lab in Cambridge.

The National Information Infrastructure (NII) could be used by government and especially corporations to acquire personal information in order to categorize individuals. This would cause the NII to become more of an information prison than superhighway. The NII would resemble a panopticon, a prison in which the guards can view all prisoners but prisoners cannot view the guards. Through the NII, corporations could act as "guards" with undue control of individuals' personal information. Individuals, the "prisoners," would be unaware how their personal information was acquired and used. At the other extreme, cryptography could electronically safeguard individuals' personal data from scrutiny. The future of personal information transmitted via the Internet probably lies somewhere between these two extremes.

The National Information Infrastructure is evolving on our screens. But behind the scenes another infrastructure is growing, one which threatens to turn the NII not into an information superhighway but into an information prison. Everyone has a different vision for the NII, from 500 channels of consumer heaven to networked egalitarian communities. There are nearly as many models for the NII as there are writers interested in the topic.

Regardless of which model holds, however, it seems clear that the NII will be a primary mechanism for the transaction of business between companies and customers and between government and citizens. A 1993 book, *The Panoptic Sort: A Political Economy of Personal Information* by Oscar Gandy,[1] attempts to paint a picture of an emerging phenomenon which affects how these transactions will be carried out.

Alan Wexelblat, "How Is the NII Like a Prison?" electronically published paper written in June 1995. Copyright 1995 by Alan Wexelblat. Reprinted with the author's permission.

This mechanism, which he calls the panoptic sort, describes an information collection and use regime which severely impacts on the privacy of, and opportunities afforded to, people in our late capitalist culture. The panoptic sort is a set of practices by government and especially by companies whereby information is gathered from people through their transactions with the commercial system. The information is then exchanged, collated, sold, compared, and subject to extensive statistical analyses.

As Gandy describes it:

> The panoptic sort is the name I have assigned to the complex technology that involves the collection, processing, and sharing of information about individuals and groups that is generated through their daily lives as citizens, employees, and consumers and is used to coordinate and control their access to the goods and services that define life in the modern capitalist economy. The panoptic sort is a system of disciplinary surveillance that is widespread but continues to expand its reach.

The goal of these activities is to enable information-holders to make predictions about the behavior of the people on whom the information was collected. The ultimate goal is to be able to sort all the people the company comes in contact with along whatever dimension of information is desired:

- How likely is this person to pay his charge bill?
- How likely is this person to become pregnant at some point in her work career?
- Does this family qualify for food stamps?

The essential element of the panoptic sort is the transaction. People, for the purpose of the sort, only exist in discrete interactions, when some exchange is made for goods or services. The prototypical transaction is the application, where the person exchanges detailed information in exchange for potential access (to a job, to medical care, etc.). People are usually not permitted to withhold information from a transaction. For example, credit card applications (even so-called pre-approved ones) will not be processed unless the applicant provides a Social Security Number (SSN). Similarly, the government now requires all children above the age of two to have an SSN if their names appear on any bank accounts or tangible assets.

A control and observation regime

In order to make discriminations such as the ones above, the decision-makers need complete information. Thus, the term *panoptic*, or all-seeing. Gandy draws the term from its earlier use by Jeremy Bentham, an English prison reformer of the previous century. Bentham proposed constructing prisons in the form of something he called a *Panopticon*. In this model, prisoners would be held in cells with glass doors arranged around a ring. At the center of the ring would be the guard tower. Important to Bentham's design was that the prisoners were isolated from each other and could not see each other, nor could they see the guards. The guards in the tower, however, could see all the prisoners without the inmates knowing they were being watched.

Gandy points out that the panoptic sort operates by essentially the same principles: our lives as consumers are opened up to scrutiny by arbitrary persons at any time for undisclosed purposes. We are atomized—treated as individual consumer-units unable to act collectively. At the same time we are prevented from knowing about the companies which observe us.

In order to make discriminations . . . , the decision-makers need complete information.

The panoptic sort also serves to extend control over unprecedented distances. Though the methods and techniques which are involved today have precedents and roots back to the beginnings of the industrial revolution, the technology in use now and in the near-NII future enables the extension of controls over global distances. Increasingly we find not just our workplaces, but our homes invaded. The transit between home and work and our vacations also face intrusion. Part of this paper was written on an airplane on which the flight steward announced that "your nightmare has come true: now you can be called in-flight." Presumably we trust that the content of these calls will not be captured and analyzed for others' advantage the way the early telegrams were read by Western Union.[2]

There are a number of consequences for people subjected to this sort of pervasive control and observation regime, not least of which is that we self-censor. People trained to expect denial (of services, credit or opportunity) will soon cease applying for more. Subject to observation at any time by unknown persons with unpredictable means of retribution, we chill our own speech and action in ways antithetical to democracy. This process is already in evidence in America today. Writer Noam Chomsky has repeatedly pointed out that official censorship is not found in America because the speech is not particularly threatening to anyone in power.

Means of operation

The panoptic sort operates by means of a three-step process: identification, classification and assessment. Identification involves the association of persons, at the time of a transaction, with an existing file of information (such as a credit or medical history). The panoptic sort not only requires us to submit increasingly detailed verifications of our identity, it requires the potential involvement of third parties merely to vouch for who/what we are; that is, our credit card companies vouch for us when we write a check, or the Department of Motor Vehicles when we buy a drink. Identification proceeds from a basis of complete distrust.

Identificative distrust has infiltrated our society to such an extent that we are all accustomed to being required to carry identicative tokens. Each of these tokens is the result of a transaction with the panopticon; each is granted to us in acknowledgment of our contribution of information to another file of information. Common "documentary tokens" (as Gandy calls them) include:

- Birth certificate
- Driver's license
- Social security card

This process of identification-via-token continues to expand. In reaction to mounting losses and falsifications associated with common tokens, new proposals are being made. The most successful of these so far is the ATM (automatic teller machine) or debit card. This card requires the user to enter a PIN (Personal Identification Number) and acts as a cash equivalent in many situations, though its on-line, real-time nature provides excellent data-gathering opportunities. Banks report losses through ATM/debit cards which are 20–30 times lower than losses associated with credit cards.[3]

The next step in this process is currently under discussion. The technology involved is the "smart" card, so named because in addition to the ability to record information (on a magnetic strip or on-board computer memory) the card contains processing power to update the stored information and do computation with it in real time. Several proposals have been put forth recently to establish a national identification system around such smart cards.[4]

Information, such as income, number of children, marital status, and so on can be used to assign people to a category such as "young, upwardly-mobile professional."

In these systems, everyone would be required to carry a card which contained potentially vast amounts of personal information about the bearer's health, financial status, physical information, residence information, and so on. In addition, the cards' memory can be used to hold recent transactional information, such as the last n purchases made or the last n banking transactions. The card could also be programmed to do real-time identification of the holder, replacing PINs with some form of biometric analysis, such as voice identification or a fingerprint.

It is worth noting that in every case, the proposal is made in response to a supposed problem: illegal immigration, welfare "cheats," national driver's licenses, access to personal medical information in an emergency. Invariably, the solution requires that we give up more of our privacy and personal information. Rather than fixing systemic causes, or looking rationally at whether these "cures" are worse than the problems they might solve, the operators of the panoptic sort use the publicity and fear associated with societal ills to expand their reach. The rational observer is left to wonder at what information from his national ID card might be made available to whom and what information might be stored on the card without the person's knowledge.[5]

Classification is "*. . . the assignment of individuals to conceptual groups on the basis of identifying information.*" Classification is fundamentally about control. Since complete detailed information on everyone is impossible, companies use increasingly small "buckets" or groupings into which people can be classified. The assertion being made is that certain discernible information, such as income, number of children, marital status, and so on can be used to assign people to a category such as "young, upwardly-mobile professional" (the original classification which led to the term "yuppie" entering the public discourse). Once people have been assigned to such groupings, their behavior can be predicted by statistical techniques applied to the group as a whole.

We must face the reality that in order for commercial transactions we initiate to be completed, we are compelled to give up information.

That is, if we can say with a high degree of confidence that all yuppies will do such-and-such (for example, buy a new car within the next three years), and we have assigned you to such a category, then we can infer that you are likely to buy a car within three years. Although professional statisticians caution against such descents from the general to the specific level, nevertheless, these predictive techniques are widely used.

Anyone who has ever dealt with a recalcitrant bureaucracy or an unyielding corporate "service" person knows how dehumanizing such a process can be. Classifications are based on particular measurements; differences which are not measured—such as individual variation—do not exist for the purposes of the panoptic sort. On an individual level, we might argue that no matter the accuracy of predictive statistics in regards to any group of people, they do not account for our individual behavior. But once assignments into these groups are made, we are no longer treated as individuals. Instead we become "welfare mothers" or "older graduate students" and are expected to conform to type. Interestingly, people seem eager to assign such labels to themselves, perhaps for the sense of community they feel when part of an identifiable group. Many groups have used such self-identification to reclaim a sense of history (e.g. the black experience in America) or assert control over terminology (e.g. gays reclaiming the word "queer").

Classification is never value-neutral; it always includes an assessment (a form of comparative classification). What makes someone "black" is often more a matter of politics than genetics or any other science. In Nazi Germany it was decided that anyone who had at least one Jewish grandparent was thereby Jewish. The income boundaries for such classifications as "upper class" or "middle class" are highly arbitrary and usually reflect the value system of the classifier (think of the phrase "middle class tax cut" and how it is used). Even such seemingly-objective classifications as medical diagnoses are subject to the vagaries of time and culture (think of the changes in psychiatric evaluations of female "hysteria" or homosexuality). Statistical techniques cannot take into account these variations.

Assessment is the process of measuring deviance or variation from the statistical norm of the class to which the assignment has been made. Assessment is a risk-avoidance procedure, a means by which the company seeks to limit its risk in relation to possible goods or services it might provide the person involved in the transaction. Assessment also encompasses the delineation of whole classes of people who may be systematically excluded or treated specially. Assessment involves computations based on probability, opportunity reduction, and loss prevention.

Assessment is based on prediction, and events today show that prediction techniques are being extended to ever-more-ambiguous domains. For example, the defense lawyers in the O.J. Simpson trial accumulated detailed profiles on potential jurors and used these profiles to "predict" which people were more likely to vote for conviction. These people were, of course, peremptorily challenged to prevent them being on the jury.

Gandy points out that there are actually three kinds of prediction and that each has its own strengths and weaknesses, but these are rarely noted:

- Statistical prediction, based on comparisons of the behavior of a group with the behavior of an individual;
- "Anamnestic" prediction, based on the person's past behavior;
- Clinical prediction, based on an expert's evaluation of the individual's behavior.

We might instinctively prefer statistical prediction because it is "scientific" and open to proof and challenge of assumptions; however, the meaning of statistics is not often so clear. The fact that a person is a member of a group which is, for example, 95% likely to buy a new car in three years does not mean that the person in question is 95% likely to do so.

From the point of view of the panoptic sort, though, this is not relevant. Concerned with optimal efficiency, it appears more efficient to (for example) prevent default than coerce those who might default or who have defaulted.

What might be done

One of the most frightening things about the panoptic sort is that it is not the result of some massive heinous centralized bureaucracy. Rather, it is a particular tragedy of the information commons, wherein each rational actor does that which seems to be in his best business interest but the overall result is the loss of something valuable. In many ways the panoptic sort is not new—it has roots at least as far back as the time-and-motion studies of the early industrial age. However, the presence of telecommunications technologies is permitting the extension of control over times and distances which were insurmountable in the past. It is no exaggeration to say that the modern multinational corporation simply could not exist without these technologies and it is these corporations which are the primary agents of the panoptic sort.

One might argue that the simple solution to the problem posed by these corporations' information gathering and to the commons tragedy of the panoptic sort in general is to control the release of information about oneself. Indeed, Gandy discusses the growing refusal of Americans to participate in marketing or opinion surveys and their resistance to official statistics-gathering, such as the US Census. Gandy points out that though awareness of privacy problems is growing, people's attitudes toward the problem and potential solutions (such as government regulation) are related to their power relative to the organizations in the panoptic sort. Generally speaking, the more power people believe they have, the less they are concerned (though this can be changed by direct personal experiences with the panoptic sort, especially negative experiences).[6]

Regardless of our power relations, we must face the reality that in order for commercial transactions we initiate to be completed, we are compelled to give up information. This is most obvious in something like a credit or loan process, which inevitably begins with an application form that demands specific and often very personal information. People may object to the gathering of such personal information. Nevertheless, Gandy points out that businesses often have what we might all agree are legitimate needs for information about the people they transact business with; the results of giving up that information, though, may turn out to be more than expected. This can be true for even the most trivial-seeming interactions.

Gandy uses a simple and compelling example: imagine that you go to a tailor to have a pair of pants fitted. It is impossible to complete this transaction without giving the tailor your measurements. But based on these measurements, it would not be difficult to detect a segment of the population which could be characterized as overweight. If your tailor was to share this information with your health insurance company, the consequences could be an increase in your insurance rates.

This example may seem silly: no one's tailor talks to his health insurance company. At least, not yet. But in the near NII future when both the tailor and the insurance company are "wired" it would be a simple matter for the insurance company to make an electronic query of the tailor and offer an incentive for the list of people whose measurements fit certain criteria. In fact, the information could be automatically transmitted as it is entered into the tailor's (insurance company–supplied) PDA [Personal Digital Assistant]. The company could then not only incorporate this information in its files, but continue to propagate it, perhaps to vendors of weight-loss plans, to defray the costs.[7]

In summary, the problem is not simple release of information; as the example above shows, we must give out some information in order to get what we need. Rather, the problem is the information's propagation to unknown parties and its application to unknown, unintended uses with unforeseeable consequences. The problem is complicated by the fact that we cannot choose to remove ourselves from participation in the panoptic sort without loss of possibly essential goods and services.

Technology and marketing

One of the most easily understood (and yet least harmful) consequences of the panoptic sort is the increasing pervasiveness and intrusion of marketing. As goods and services proliferate in a capitalist culture, an increasing effort must be made by purveyors to bring their particular product to the attention of potential customers.

Advertisers are always seeking to improve the efficiency of their marketing. Currently, direct-marketing firms which mail to lists of "prospects" consider a 3–4% return rate to be very successful. That means that for every potential customer they contact, they must intrude on and annoy to some degree 30–50 other people. The ability to target that 3–4% beforehand is a primary motivation in the panoptic collection of information. We might argue on a detailed basis whether we feel it is desirable for advertisers to have this or that level of information about us. One side might argue that having better information reduces the level of intrusion into our lives; the other might argue that personal information is the property of the person about whom it speaks and that people should be able to choose what information they release to whom.

However, Gandy points out that it is worth asking the larger question of why we must have this debate in the first place. That is, we should consider the relationship of technology to marketing (and to capitalist culture at large). Technology is not neutral; it is introduced by parties with interests to further and, in turn, it has ripple effects which can be only dimly foreseen.

We cannot choose to remove ourselves from participation in the panoptic sort without loss of possibly essential goods and services.

One obvious example is the Internet itself: originally conceived as a network for researchers to exchange scientific information, it instead became primarily a rapid-communications medium and a means of establishing non-geographical communities. However, while the street has its own uses for things, often it is the humans who must be reshaped to accommodate the technology. The debate about the acceptable level of advertiser knowledge and intrusion would not be occurring without our having previously been conditioned to accept a continual bombardment of advertising. This subtle reworking of people is also a part of the panoptic process.

Gandy shows that this process, too, has roots in the earliest parts of the Industrial Age (and in fact significantly pre-dates advertising). He cites and quotes Jacques Ellul, an analyst of technology.[8] Ellul traces the mechanization of the production of bread, pointing out that an attribute of the wheat made it difficult for the machines to produce bread which was like that baked pre-machine. Rather than adapting the machines, industrialists set about to create a demand for a new kind of bread. The goal was efficient (that is, profitable for the owners of the bread-making machines) production and if people had to be reshaped for efficiency, so be it.

This process has become so ingrained in our culture that we no longer recognize it. As we witness the transformation of the Internet into a marketing medium and locus of business transactions, we should remember how far this process has come. Gandy quotes the modern analyst David Lovekin on this:

> Thus, a simple food like potatoes becomes Tater-Tots, something that is not clearly food at all and that contains elements of no clearly known nutritional value. What is clear is that each piece is made to look like the other pieces, identities which are also different, new. McDonald's markets and produces sameness. . . . To understand fast food, a purely

technological phenomenon, one must look to the walls and notice the pictures of the food. One buys the picture, which will never nourish, but which will always keep the customer coming back for more, the ever-perfect, indeed, the same hamburger, designed in the laboratory and cooked by computers.[9]

As we watch the development of Web sites promoting ever more unrealistic images of companies and their products, it is both an interesting game and a frightening prospect to imagine what new products we are being conditioned to accept. We see the beginnings of the intrusions of panoptic data gathering on the Web. Sites maintain (and sometimes publish) information about the hosts that connect to them. Many sites require users to "register" or "sign in," once again enforcing the transactional model of information gathering.

As with any analysis of the present situation and associated trends, the range of possible futures that could be developed is quite large. However, we can characterize a spectrum along which the future probably lies by examining its extreme ends. Here are two futures which lie at opposite ends of a realm of possible results. The first is The Panopticon, the second Cryptoprivacy.

The panopticon

This scenario can be seen as the result of momentum, or inertia, rather than the influence of any specific set of factors. As noted above, the panoptic sort is the result of individual (rational) actors working to further what each sees as his own best interest, his most efficient operation.

In this scenario, nothing much changes: companies continue to migrate to places (both real and electronic) where they are most unencumbered by the regulation of increasingly-irrelevant governments. Consumers, anesthetized by media, indifferent to the slow erosion of rights they do not understand, silently acquiesce to the process. Governments may even abet the process, as they chase what Bruce Sterling characterized as "The Four Horsemen of the Modern Apocalypse": terrorists, child pornographers, drug kingpins, and the Mafia.[10] It is notable that the response to each public tragedy or threat in modern America seems to involve a call for citizens to surrender more of their rights. Recently, we have seen such calls for surrender in response to the Oklahoma bombing [of the Alfred P. Murrah Federal Building in 1995] and in response to the potential availability of pornography on the Internet.

Privacy is, after all, a notion contextualized by social time and place, and legal history. The modern conception of privacy can be traced back to a law review article published in 1890 by Samuel D. Warren and Louis D. Brandeis, titled "The Right to Privacy." In the future, we may reconceive privacy as something less related to information. Perhaps privacy will come to mean something like the ability to keep our moment-to-moment thoughts from being known by others.[11]

If this conception seems strange, remember the example of the tailor. In a truly networked nation, it seems logical to assume that any entity which can communicate information will do so. Corporations' drive for efficiency will provide us with an ever-growing stream of products customized for our specific situations, manufactured just in time to meet needs we didn't even know we had.

Of course, information will be provided to us as well. In response to our manufactured needs, we will be fed a steady diet of 500+ channels, each with its content carefully labeled to avoid potentially offending anyone, just as CDs and soon video games are labeled and rated. These ratings will be the result of panoptic classifications and the people who buy them can expect to have their preferences recorded and analyzed so that the next offerings to reach their homes, cars and offices will be closer to their expected tastes and values.

In this version of the future, business efficiency is paramount. All other needs are subsumed to the desire to have the most successful competitive capitalist structure. Neither businesses nor governments need to enact new policies for this scenario to come to pass; it does not depend on any particular new technological advances. All that is required is that we do nothing, that we continue to make decisions as they are made today, that we extend current technological advancements to more sectors of society.

The consequences of this scenario would be unnoticeable. Remember that the panoptic sort does not advance with speed; rather it moves in cautious increments, taking advantage of the willingness of people to go along with things that appear to be in everyone's best capitalistic interest. All that would happen is that our grandchildren would listen to our stories of the "old days" and shake their heads amusedly.

Cryptoprivacy

With the lessening dominance of mass media and consequent reduction in its tendency to homogenize opinion and enforce compliance with current power structures, it is interesting to speculate on the possible re-emergence of a critical thought consciousness in American political discourse. Such a consciousness, presumably similar to that raised after the abuses of Watergate were made known, might lead to modification or lessening of the panoptic sort. Gandy, in reporting his studies of corporate attitudes and policies, notes that corporations are most acutely aware of public opinion and possible governmental regulation. If these factors appear to be favoring a move toward greater regulation, corporations respond by preemptively changing their policies. Presumably, they believe that voluntary changes will both ameliorate negative opinions and will be less severe than external regulation or public outcry. We might hope that Net-based political consciousness would motivate such changes.

Sadly it seems increasingly unlikely that this will happen. Though the Net provides a potential medium for discourse and consciousness-raising dialog, it has proved incapable of making an organized response beyond single issues (such as the alerts found at the EFF [Electronic Freedom Foundation] Web site). Though the Net is worldwide, the most effective use of the medium has been community networks used to address town- or local-level issues and dialog.

While it is always dangerous to hope that technology will provide answers or solutions to social problems, it does seem that we are on the verge of seeing a technology emerge which could revolutionize the power relationship between companies and individuals.[12] This technology, ubiquitous easy public-key encryption, would permit individuals to maintain more control over their personal information. This technology and its implications are being investigated, publicized, and hotly debated by a group of hackers, mathematicians, libertarians, and social reformers loosely referred to as cypherpunks.[13]

Cryptography itself is at least as old as Julius Caesar. Loosely speaking, encryption is the process of taking a text X and applying a function f to it to produce a cyphertext Y. The reverse process is to take Y and apply another function g to decrypt it and get X back. A major problem in the past has been that f depends on a key k such that if I know f and I find out k then I can do the decryption. Most such functions are what is known as *invertible*. An obvious solution is to use non-invertible functions; however, these are still susceptible to key loss.

It is both an interesting game and a frightening prospect to imagine what new products we are being conditioned to accept.

This problem was solved by three mathematicians: Ron Rivest, Adi Shamir, and Leonard Adleman. They patented a technique for splitting k into two parts, one public and one private.[14] The functions associated with these keys are constructed such that if I have someone's public key and Y, I still cannot retrieve the original message. Only the owner of the private key can decrypt the message. The best-known implementation of the RSA algorithms is Phil Zimmerman's program called PGP (Pretty Good Privacy).[15] For the rest of this scenario I will use PGP as a synonym for public key encryption.

The implications of this technology are potentially enormous; for the purposes of this future scenario, we will assume they are developed. The first implication is that communication can be secure from outside intrusions. As noted above, one of the most insidious effects of panoptic surveillance is that people begin to self-censor. However, if we weaken the ability of outsiders to monitor our speech, then we can speak more freely. Of course, speech in a public forum is still public and potentially monitored.

However, one of the unusual conditions of public speech on the Net is that it is speech identified with a person by virtue of an electronic address. That address can also be concealed; indeed, the cypherpunks have already set up a network of anonymous remailers which permit people to send email and post messages anonymously. We can imagine that this network will be extended in the future to permit anonymous transmission of all kinds of information. Conversely, in cases where it is important that speakers be reliably identified, these networks can refuse to transmit messages which are not validated by the proper keys. In cases such as pronouncements from public officials, this can be critically important.

The second implication of public-key cryptography is that people can generate unique signatures. In particular, given a document and a private key, an author can produce a signature (a block of numbers) which is unforgeable and undeniable. That is, no other key will produce that signature, and in addition, any change to the message will produce a different signature. Thus, tampering and forgery are easily detected. Verification is simple and can be done by anyone with access to the author's public key, which can be freely distributed.

This capability is the converse of the first; what we say can be identified with us to a degree of certainty at least equal to that provided by physical signatures. Remember that one of the fundamental operations of the panoptic sort is identification—people are identified with file records and people are trained to carry and supply identificative tokens which reveal intimate physical information such as height, weight, and birth date. PGP allows people to be identified by their public and private keys. No necessary connection exists between a person and a key pair—people can have as many key pairs as they need, companies can generate new key pairs for each customer if they so choose.

Ultimately, an identity *is* a key-pair. Alan-Wexelblat-who-works-for-MIT is not precisely the same person as Alan-Wexelblat-who-buys-Macintosh-computers. The importance of making this distinction can be seen in the "disclaimers" regularly made in e-mail and Usenet postings by people who wish it to be known that they are speaking solely for themselves and not for an organization which might be attached to their name.

Keys themselves can be signed. A person may have any number of other signatories to his key. These people, in effect, testify that this key belongs to this person. They, in turn, can have their keys signed. The result is what is referred to as a "web of trust" in which I may not directly know the holder of a given key, but I may know someone who knows him or someone who knows someone who knows him.

Such chains, which might be thought to be potentially quite long, are limited by the principle that all people in the world are connected by a chain of no more than six people. In addition, we can imagine that well-known institutions such as MIT would establish key-signatory authorities. Since these institutions must verify personal identity before admitting people, they can in turn testify to the identity of these people to any who want to know by signing their key. This replicates today's identificative structures wherein agents accept particular tokens because they trust that the agencies which issue those tokens have done the work necessary to establish that the bearer is indeed the person specified.

However, by having a trustworthy token with no connection to myself, I break one of the fundamental connections of the panoptic sort: the association between a person and his identification. This, in itself, is not necessarily a significant disruption to the panoptic sort, but it does move in the right direction.

Digital cash

The final implication of public key encryption is the one which might have the most impact: digital cash.[16] That is, in a future where this technology is widely used, it will be possible to buy and sell goods and services over the network with "coins" which are as valid as physical money is today, as unforgeable as the digital signatures described above and as anonymous as encrypted messages.

The significance of this advance for disruption of the panoptic sort, and for government in general, is enormous. Digital cash is like physical cash in that it is potentially untraceable. With digital cash I can pay for goods and services with the surety of the bank or other organization which issued the digital coins, and yet not have to reveal anything at all about myself. This strikes directly at the heart of the panoptic sort.

The recourse to cash is not new. In today's society, those who are most excluded from the benefits of society are most likely to resort to using cash. In many cases, it is their only recourse—denied credit, unable to prove themselves sufficiently to make checks acceptable, they must pay with cash (often after paying exorbitant fees for converting their payroll or government checks to cash). In doing so, they do not create transaction records and do not "build up credit." In a negative sense, it can be seen as a process which keeps poorer people (or people who have bad credit or who have declared bankruptcy or whatever) from taking advantage of many of the services available to others. In a positive sense, it can be seen as a way to exempt oneself from the panoptic sort. Digital cash would make it possible for people of all means to exempt themselves to a significant degree.

Public-key encryption would permit individuals to maintain more control over their personal information.

This scenario supposes a series of radical changes in governmental policy. At present, US cryptographic policy is strongly opposed to the widespread use of public key encryption. Governmental agencies (particularly the FBI) would have to accept the idea that citizens could have conversations and hold information to which the government would potentially have no access. Currently, the government's approach centers on escrowed keys, export restrictions on cryptographic information (which is treated as munitions), and wiretap capabilities built into the telecommunications system (and presumably into the NII).

Businesses would also have to change their model of contact with customers. Currently, businesses feel compelled to "push" their information out to potential customers. To do that efficiently they require the ever more detailed information of the panoptic sort. However, if that information is not available, businesses would have to adopt more of a "storefront" approach where they advertise only their general existence and types of goods and wait for potential customers to come to them. This model is, to some degree, what is practiced today on the World Wide Web.

Legal changes would also have to occur to recognize a digital signature as valid. It is likely, however, that practice would lead legislation in this case—the law has often recognized technological changes as they prove themselves. For example, the changes which allow DNA "fingerprinting" to be admitted as evidence; there are as yet no federal laws on DNA use in court, but it is becoming accepted practice. Therefore, this scenario assumes that a series of legal cases have built up the necessary precedents for digital signatures to have the force of law.

The most important aspect of cryptoprivacy is also the one which would require the most changes. For digital money to become an everyday reality could require significant legislative changes; the ability to make money is one of the most closely-held powers of any sovereign state. David Chaum, the inventor of digital cash, has set up the first company to issue and redeem DigiBucks, as they are called.

Currently, on-line means that things are more accessible to the panoptic sort.

While it is highly unlikely that governments will give up their power to mint money, our economy has moved away from minted money as the primary means of exchange. Credit cards proliferate, as do electronic funds transfers. The IRS collects most of its taxes from corporations in electronic form; vast sums are transferred between banks and the Federal Reserve digitally. The fact that consumers still use physical monetary tokens is merely an indication that the electronic funds part of the NII still has not been wired up to the "last mile"—i.e. each person's house. This is changing, however, as personal financial programs such as Intuit's Quicken encourage electronic payments and personal tax preparation programs encourage electronic filing.

Chaum's company, DigiCash, has been set up in the Netherlands. However, most of its suppliers and users are in the United States. This points up one of the most troubling consequences of this scenario for the government. As noted above, corporations have historically been quite willing to change locations ("move offshore") in order to provide more favorable environments for themselves. If digital cash becomes widely accepted and the country's consumer transactions go electronic, then government may have tremendous trouble accepting an anonymous system such as DigiCash. Currently, on-line means that things are more accessible to the panoptic sort. Credit records, electronic payments and so on all carry critical identificative information. Digital cash does not. It is, in effect, a virtually invisible economy and one which could spell the end of government's ability to monitor and collect taxes.

Between two extremes

This article has described the outlines of a pervasive practice of control, the panoptic sort. This practice is not a conspiracy of any person or group; rather, it is a tragedy of the information commons where each actor works in his own best interest and the result is something undesirable for all of us. The panoptic sort works to control us by shaping our behaviors, our expectations, as well as our reactions to society and to each other.

The goal of this control is optimum efficiency, expressed in terms of maximizing business profitability. The techniques of the sort are not particularly new, but the technology of the network era allows unprecedented extensions of control into every aspect of our lives. This very extension is itself undesirable, as it conflicts with our modern notions of privacy.

Two possible outcomes have been described, providing endpoints on a spectrum of possibilities. In one extreme case, nothing changes and we sink slowly into an information panopticon. In the other, everything changes and we establish technological barriers to protect ourselves. In reality, the future probably lies somewhere in between these two extremes. Governments may take some steps to protect individuals' privacy as might the people themselves. Corporations may realize that it is not in their best interest to continually intrude and could exercise some measure of self-restraint.

Fundamentally, though, the most important question is what we think our society is good for. If we allow the panoptic sort to continue we are resigning ourselves to a world in which corporate efficiency is the highest goal we can aspire to. Somehow, there seems to be something wrong with that idea.

Notes

1. Gandy, Oscar. *The Panoptic Sort: A Political Economy of Personal Information*, Westview Press, 1993.

2. Salomon, R. "A History of Railroads and Telecommunications," lecture given to [an MIT class], April 1995.

3. Svigals, Jerome. "Smart Cards—a Critical Decision Point," *Journal of Retail Banking*, vol 19, no. 1, Spring 1987.

4. The commissioner of the IRS, in discussing the potential impact of on-line financial transactions, raised the possibility of "real-time tax collection" whereby the IRS would figure for you, and collect from you, your taxes as you made each financial transaction. Other such proposals have come from an alliance of state motor vehicle agencies and auto insurers, from the Social Security Administration, and frequently from the speeches of Vice President Al Gore, who is a champion of the idea that everyone carry his medical history around with him at all times.

5. At the most recent Computers, Freedom, and Privacy conference, opponents of the national ID card proposals were distributing buttons with Stars of David on them and the slogan "Is your Jew bit set?" Though this example is, perhaps, a bit hyperbolic, it does not seem at all extreme to assume that people's medical records would include information about such sensitive matters as pregnancy status, psychiatric diagnoses, and other information which we would not want given out without our knowledge and consent. A national ID card with such information on it would mean giving away our entire medical histories to anyone to whom we identified ourselves.

6. Gandy also performs an incisive analysis of the role of the media in affecting public attitudes toward the panoptic sort. There is not space in the paper to discuss his research, but his conclusion is worth noting: "The mass media play a critical role in informing people about the risks and dangers [. . .] in their relations with the institutions of business and government. A critical role played by the mass media, especially television, is the reinforcing of a compliance with the dominant values that legitimate the operation of the panoptic sort."

7. If you still think this example is silly, consider the following: "Microsoft officials confirm that beta versions of Windows 95 include a small viral routine called Registration Wizard. It interrogates every system on a network gathering intelligence on what software is being run on which machine. It then creates a complete listing of both Microsoft's and competi-

tors' products by machine, which it reports to Microsoft when customers sign up for Microsoft's Network Services. Customers must actively disable the routine if they don't want it to run." *Information Week*, May 22, 1995.

8. Ellul, Jacques. *Propaganda: The Formation of Men's Attitudes* (trans. K. Lellen & J. Lerner), Vintage Books, 1973.

9. Lovekin, David. *Technique, Discourse and Consciousness: An Introduction to the Philosophy of Jacques Ellul*, Lehigh University Press, 1991.

10. Sterling, Bruce. Address given to the Third Annual Conference on Computers, Freedom, and Privacy, CFP'93.

11. I am indebted to the author Pat Cadigan for this idea.

12. Sterling showed no such reluctance in his closing remarks at CFP'94 where he referred to "*. . . the white-hot volcano of technological advance in the direct path of a Cold War glacier that has previously crushed everything in its way.*"

13. "Crypto Rebels," *Wired*, vol. 1, no. 2.

14. The technique, described in detail in RSA's FAQ is based on multiplication of large prime numbers. A large enough (e.g. 1,024 bits) key cannot be factored with existing computers in any reasonable amount of time, thus protecting the keys from brute-force attacks. Keys are still susceptible to loss—a computer trojan horse could capture a key as it was used—or compromise. Courts will surely soon issue a warrant compelling someone to give up his private key. But these issues are outside the scope of this paper. For a more detailed discussion of cryptographic issues, the multi-part Usenet cryptography FAQ is quite helpful.

15. Zimmerman, Phil. *The Official PGP User's Guide*, MIT Press, 1995. See also the EFF's PGP information archive.

16. Chaum, David. "Achieving Electronic Privacy," *Scientific American*, August 1992.

8

The Internet Will Impair Education

Chaitram Ramphal

Chaitram Ramphal is a teacher's education student at York University in Toronto, Canada.

Education requires discussion between teachers and students. But computers and the Internet detract from such discussion. This disruption of the student-teacher relationship will cause students to become disinterested in education and to be confused about their place in society and about their future. Influenced by the Internet, learning will no longer be equated with understanding and knowledge, but rather with acquiring information. The Internet threatens to replace teachers as the focal point of education, but it cannot teach important values such as discipline, responsibility, and cooperation.

One can best open discussion of the effect of the Internet on education by referring to the judgement of Thamus. Imagine Theuth [Thamus and Theuth were Egyptian gods], having invented the Internet, showing it to Thamus. He might have introduced the Internet in the same way that he had introduced writing: "Here is an accomplishment, my lord the King, that will improve the wisdom of all mankind. I have discovered a sure receipt for memory and wisdom." Theuth might also have added: "I have also found a truly new way to carry on a discussion. Knowledge and wisdom can be transmitted in a truly remarkable way. The electronic discourses made possible will ensure the protection of democracy." To this Thamus might have replied: "It is in this; you who are the the father of the Internet, out of fondness for your own off-spring attribute to it quite the opposite of its real function. Your pupils will have the reputation for wisdom without the reality: they will receive a quantity of information without proper instruction, and in consequence be thought of as very knowledgeable when for the most part they are quite ignorant. And because they are filled with the conceit of wisdom instead of real wisdom they will be a burden to society. As for democracy, the detachment of di-

Chaitram Ramphal, "The Internet's Effect on Education," an electronically published paper written in November 1996. Copyright 1996 by Chaitram Ramphal. Reprinted with the author's permission.

rect human involvement in discourses on the Internet will destroy democracy."

In order to discuss the effect of the Internet on education, one must first look at the purpose of education. In Neil Postman's *End of Education*, he proposed that one purpose of education is to change the student, so that the student will become a different person because of what he has learned. Education needs a purpose and clarity to learning—students must know what they should be learning, and why they are learning it. Students need to find inner meaning to what they are learning, so that they will have the motivation to learn, and so that they can fit that into their personal lives. Postman referred to this as the students (and teachers) needing a "god" to serve. This "god" could be anything powerful enough to underline all educational themes. For example, it could be Saving the Planet, Discussion of Human Development, Understanding the World We Live In, or Personal Development. Recently, these gods are slowly being dismantled from the educational system. These gods depend on free human discussion to exist. The computer and the Internet detract from this human discussion; students will become too demoralized and bored to care for any of these gods. The computer and the Internet will cause the final destruction of these gods. With no powerful gods to serve, the student will have no clear idea of his place in society, there is no vision of past or future, no organizing principles, and schools will become purposeless. This leads to a barren culture, where there is an abundance of drugs, suicide, and tribalism.

New demi-gods

However, the Internet introduces new "demi-gods" to education. This is the god of Technology. This god teaches that technology is power, and that human beings are replaceable by machines. In this god's world, technological progress is mistaken for human progress. So that the faster you can surf the Internet, the better you are. In this world, educators no longer provide reasons for learning; they are merely responsible for providing new methods for learning—finding new ways to apply technology to "learning." The meaning of Learning itself will change. Learning will no longer mean Understanding and Knowledge, but instead it will mean Giving Information. This is truly the Conceit of Wisdom, where information is mistaken for knowledge.

The Internet threatens to push teachers into the sidelines and place itself as the heart of education.

But the god of Technology has an evil side to it. This is the god of Economic Utility. This god strikes at the very psyche of the student, and the values of the student are changed forever. This god teaches that the purpose of education is to get a good job. The person is judged by what he does, and he who earns the most money is the best. But there is still a more heinous god standing behind; this is the god of Consumerism. This god tells the student that the person who dies with the most toys wins, that life is made worthwhile by buying things. Why does the Internet fit so perfectly in with these gods? Because these are the gods that created the Internet in the first place. The Internet is hostile to education. It shifts attention from the teacher to itself, and its ultimate agenda is to substitute some master formula that will take the place of resourcefulness and competence of teachers. Proponents, such as Lewis Perelman in his book *School's Out*, argue that the Internet has made schools irrelevant.

Exactly what will the Internet take away from education? What will it change? These questions need to be discussed before we rush headlong into this new technology. One thing is for sure, the Internet threatens to push teachers into the sidelines and place itself as the heart of education. It threatens to redefine education itself. But the replacement of teachers by the Internet will be an irreparable loss. Teachers teach the students how to behave in society, how to respect others. These are values, basic values in a democratic society, and cannot be taught by computers; they must be experienced by the students. Students need discipline and self-restraint to behave in a group. The school, functioning as a collection of individuals, teaches cohesion and responsibility. The Internet cannot teach these things. It is the greatest threat to democracy that there ever was. Personal human involvement has always been a critical part of education. Can the Internet help little Mary with the impending divorce of her parents? It will probably do more harm than good, for Mary will probably seek refuge in one of the less than healthy sites. How will the Internet respond to a child with low self-esteem? Will the Internet teach tolerance? As the Internet distracts attention from these problems, they will get more serious, and eventually spill over into the society. Society will then blame education for not catching it in time. Education will then be pushed further into the sidelines with the attitude that "if you have a problem, then let the Internet solve it." Perhaps counsellors will become available over the Internet to solve students' problems.

In the Internet, information takes the place of judgement. Students are taught to retrieve and regurgitate information instead of developing analytic skills.

9

Inadequate Security Will Threaten Internet Commerce

Stephen Cobb

Stephen Cobb is the director of special projects for the National Computer Security Association, a Carlisle, Pennsylvania, organization that works to improve the security of computer users' information systems.

The Internet is attracting tremendous interest among businesses and consumers. Making Internet commerce secure is one of the biggest challenges facing information security experts. Security problems affect three areas of Internet commerce: credit card transactions, encrypted transactions between systems, and verification of the authenticity of communications. Security standards for Internet transactions will not automatically result in secure exchanges. Electronic vandalism, reliability and performance problems, and security infractions committed by employees are security issues that will continue to require attention.

Information security or infosec is about protecting three things: the confidentiality, integrity, and availability of data. Securing Internet commerce is probably the biggest challenge that infosec professionals have yet faced. In 1993, Internet commerce did not exist. Today it is attracting enormous financial interest. Investors are enthusiastically backing companies that promise to deliver the hardware and software which Internet commerce requires. Companies are investing in purchases of hardware and software to permit them to engage in Internet commerce. But what is Internet commerce?

For many companies, Internet commerce means taking credit card orders from customers shopping electronic catalogs on the World Wide Web [WWW]. For others Internet commerce means dealing electronically with clients and suppliers, as an alternative to private, leased-line electronic document interchange (EDI over Value Added Networks or VANs). This use of the Internet is sometimes called a Virtual Private Network

Stephen Cobb, "Security Issues in Internet Commerce," white paper of the National Computer Security Association; ©1996. Reprinted by permission of the author and the National Computer Security Association.

(VPN) or tunneling. A third area of Internet commerce, which overlaps both of the others and includes areas largely unexplored, is digital authentication (of anything from contracts and invoices to photographs and sound bites).

The issues involved in Internet commerce affect companies large and small. As of January 1996, half of all businesses with more than 1,000 employees had at least one Web site, according to a Yankee Group survey (which also found that nearly two-thirds of all companies with Web sites had less than 100 employees). The Internet is attractive to smaller companies because it enables them to reach a wide audience/market with a presence as impressive as that created by much larger entities. At the same time, most major corporations see enough potential to invest significant dollars (over $500,000 per company in the 1,000 employee plus category).

The security problems affecting the three areas of Internet commerce are summarized in the following three sections.

Credit card transactions

There is considerable, and justifiable, fear that confidential information, such as credit cards and personal details, could be intercepted during transmission over the Internet, for example when submitting an order form on the Web. The challenge is to transmit and receive information over the Internet while insuring that:

- it is inaccessible to anyone but sender and receiver (privacy),
- it has not been changed during transmission (integrity),
- the receiver can be sure it came from the sender (authenticity),
- the sender can be sure the receiver is genuine (non-fabrication),
- the sender cannot deny he or she sent it (non-repudiation).

Without special software, all Internet traffic travels "in the clear" and so anyone who monitors traffic can read it. This form of "attack" is relatively easy to perpetrate using freely available "packet sniffing" software since the Internet has traditionally been a very "open" network.

If you use the "trace route" command from a Unix workstation that is communicating across the Internet you can see how many different systems the data passes through on the way from client to server. At the beginning and end of the list you will probably see "local providers" or ISPs (Internet Service Providers). Most of these are considered "easy targets" by hackers, particularly if the ISP has servers on a college campus. In between you will probably see several machines operated by big name communications providers, such as Sprint or MCI. These may be more secure, but illegal penetration of even these systems poses "no problem" to some hackers.

Typically, a sniffing attack proceeds by compromising a local ISP at one end of the transmission. No special physical access is required (it is also possible to eavesdrop using network diagnostic hardware if you have physical access to the network cabling). Passwords and credit cards can be distinguished from the rest of the traffic using simple pattern matching algorithms. The defense against this type of attack is to encrypt the traffic, or at least that portion which contains the sensitive data. However, encryption incurs performance overhead and requires coordination between legitimate parties to the communication. In commercial terms, such coordination requires widespread standards for secured transactions, which have been slow to emerge.

Note that protecting transactions is only one element of the secure transaction problem. Once confidential information has been received from a client it must be protected on the server. Currently, Web servers are among the softest targets for hackers, largely due to the immaturity of the technology (for details download and read Lincoln Stein's excellent World Wide Web Security FAQ from www.ncsa.com).[1] The standard security advice for Web servers is to treat the machine as a sacrificial lamb, i.e. unconnected to any in-house networks and regularly backed up in order to recover from the inevitable attacks. However, many Web applications now in vogue require that the Web server interact with company databases, necessitating a link to internal networks. This link then becomes a pathway into your systems from your Web site. While firewall technology can help to block this path, it is seldom installed or maintained effectively and does not protect many Web services.[2]

Virtual private networks

This is a specialized form of encrypted Internet transaction allowing a secure channel (or tunnel) to be established between two systems for the purposes of electronic data interchange. This differs from credit card and consumer ordering transactions in that the volume of data between the two parties is greater and the two parties are well known to each other. This means that complex and proprietary encryption and authentication techniques can be used since there is no pretense to offer universal connectivity through this channel.

Despite the potential for greater security, the VPN is still a worrying development from a security perspective. For a start there is the attention that this "increased security" will attract from hackers and cypherpunks,[3] possibly leading to embarrassing or even costly cracking of codes. However, even if the encryption techniques employed by the digital tunneling systems currently on the market or under development prove to be very powerful, thus insuring confidentiality and availability of data, this still leaves the third aspect of security, availability.

For the foreseeable future there is huge potential for denial of service attacks on VPNs. There are currently hundreds of retail operations that depend upon just-in-time inventory replacement. The data that triggers the delivery from the manufacturer travels electronically from the store, currently over private lines. If public lines, i.e. the Internet, are used, the potential for intentional disruption is enormous, not to mention the current lack of protection against accidental service outages.

Digital certification

This area will continue to grow in importance as companies seek trusted third parties to hold digital certificates that can be used to electronically prove the identities of message senders and receivers, the integrity of documents (e.g. that an invoice has not been changed) and even the validity of digital media, such as sound recordings, photographs, and so on (e.g. if crime scene photographers switch to digital cameras someone will need to verify that the images presented in court are the same as those originally taken at the scene).

While the cryptographic basis of these mechanisms is impressive, they leave open several possible areas of exploitation in terms of sharp practice, fraud, extortion, and so on. It is not fanciful to imagine the value of digital certificates reaching a point where the temptation to betray trust, which rests upon less-than-perfect humans, will be considerable.

Apart from the specific problems described above, there are general obstacles to Internet commerce, presented in the following sections.

The frontier problem

This can be summed up by saying "Nobody has ever done this before." In other words, this is a new field of knowledge, a genuine electronic frontier. There are some similarities with other areas of experience, such as:

- conventional credit and debit card payment/guarantee schemes,
- electronic document interchange or EDI systems,
- traditional data protection methods,
- and everyday infosecurity threat management.

But there are also several significant factors which make commercial transactions on the Internet a "whole new ball game." These include:

- the global factor, the need to conduct transactions across international borders, encompassing a wide range of attitudes to commerce and encryption,
- the scale factor, the realization that the Internet is a bigger network than anything else we have encountered, by quantum factors (and this at a time when many companies are only just realizing that their internal networks have grown incomprehensibly complex),
- the big brain factor, the unprecedented amount of brain power that the Internet can focus on any proposed solution, virtually eliminating the prospect of proprietary solutions, and ensuring that any solution will have to evolve over time,
- and finally, perhaps most importantly, the inherent insecurity of the Internet, which was not designed with secure transactions in mind, and which has, for many years, been the playground of hackers.

In the face of massive enthusiasm for this new technology the security professional must stress that "all security is relative" and advise that any practical answer to these problems has to be a compromise between vulnerability and risk (e.g. there are some vulnerabilities which only a handful of people are currently skilled enough to exploit, which implies that the likelihood of the vulnerability materializing as an actual threat is relatively minor). The assessment of each threat must be weighed against what is at stake, the exposure faced by proceeding with the knowledge that some attacks are possible.

This takes system managers into the area of due diligence and liability. If someone steals credit card information from your site, you had better be able to document your defenses and the basis for deciding that they were adequate. Current technologies for encrypting Web transactions don't necessarily protect customer or company data that sits on the Web server, which is often relatively easy to attack.

Note that liability extends beyond traditional areas. What if your Internet servers are used as a jumping off point for a hacker attack on another company? What if your corporate image is defaced by an attack on your Web content? What if your Web presence creates unexpected responsibilities (as, for example, in the case of Volvo, which found it had a legal obligation to answer all email complaints)?

The market problem

The limitations of current Internet transaction technology are frustrating because we know that powerful encryption exists with which to insure the confidentiality, integrity, authenticity, and non-repudiation of data. These include private key encryption (e.g. Triple DES [Data Encryption Standard], IDEA [International Data Encryption Algorithm], Blowfish, RC4, and RC5), plus public key encryption (e.g. RSA, SEEK, PGP [Pretty Good Privacy], and ECC). However, deployment of this technology is hampered by market forces, which apply immense pressure on companies to release products and create continually shifting alliances between groups of companies hoping to carve up the market.

Technically speaking, there is a big difference between an algorithm and its implementation. To quote leading cryptographer Bruce Schneier: "The technology is not weak in and of itself, it is just badly implemented."[4] Software engineers work for companies that have marketing departments with bottom lines. We will always need to be concerned about quality standards when encryption systems are developed under these circumstances. We have already seen holes in schemes, such as Secure Sockets Layer (SSL), arising not from weaknesses in the underlying encryption technology, but from shortcomings in the implementation.

Another market-related problem has been the lack of broad standards for secure transactions due to the posturing of competing commercial entities. Two technologies, SSL and SHTTP, were headed for broad acceptance, until Visa, MasterCard and Microsoft entered the fray (Microsoft pushing PCT or Private Communication Technology). Historically speaking, the Internet was built upon public domain code, free software, and mutual co-operation in an academic/research environment.[5]

Currently, Web servers are among the softest targets for hackers, largely due to the immaturity of the technology.

Within this open, Unix-based culture, security evolved dialectically between programmers who openly devised, discussed, and addressed threats and vulnerabilities. Standards tended to emerge through co-operation and consensus. Proposed security measures or operating system enhancements were subject to public scrutiny. Software flaws, including those in production systems, were widely broadcast and openly discussed. Today the Internet lies between the land of the mainframe and the realm of the desktop, both of which have strongly proprietary cultures, with standards tending to emerge through the conflict of the market place, rather than consensus, with business practices sometimes so aggressive that they invite the scrutiny of governments (first IBM, then Microsoft).

In the desktop realm, where the largest number of users now operate, security has largely been ignored. Desktop operating systems are notoriously lacking in security features and most desktop machines are inherently insecure. While the network operating systems with which PCs are connected have the ability to implement some sophisticated security measures, the network cannot retrofit security onto the desktop and in several recent cases we have seen the desktop blow new holes in the network.[6]

So, these three cultures, UNIX, Mainframe, and Desktop, are converging on the Internet at a time when security of transactions and data is higher than ever before in the consciousness of users (in other words, users are now demanding greater security than ever before, in more places than ever before). History suggests that open, non-proprietary standards are the key to future growth of the Internet. Tending to confirm this is the dismal track record of the largest player in the proprietary, PC-based world.[7]

Current technologies for encrypting Web transactions don't necessarily protect customer or company data that sits on the Web server, which is often relatively easy to attack.

In 1995 we stated that only an open security architecture, subject to intense testing and scrutiny, free from licensing fees and other vested interests, could serve as the basis for Internet security standards (while noting that there will be plenty of opportunity for competing proprietary implementations and profit-making programs, once safe Internet transaction mechanisms are in place). We are happy to report that there have been positive moves in this direction.

The government problem

Through the International Traffic in Arms Regulations (ITAR), the U.S. government exercises control over the export of "strong" cryptography.[8] While refusing to define "strong" the government regularly denies export licenses to products, such as database software, that use encryption (some exceptions are banking and cryptography used for authentication rather than encryption). Among the effects is a large negative financial impact on U.S. software companies who cannot export the same programs that they sell domestically. As William Hugh Murray observes, "Since cryptography is heavily used across borders, American vendors of cryptography or software that uses it, operate at a competitive disadvantage because of these controls."[9]

Of course, some countries are beyond the reach of the U.S. government and cryptographic software flourishes in such places. You can buy full 128-bit stream ciphers and 56-bit DES software on the streets of Moscow. You can download Triple-DES encryption programs from sites on the Internet. Several Swiss companies are happy to supply products based on the very powerful, and widely documented, 128-bit IDEA algorithm. Bruce Schneier has described how to program many powerful algorithms in his book, *Applied Cryptography.*[10]

Since imports of powerful encryption into the U.S. are not as restricted as exports, U.S. companies that need secure transactions between countries may opt to obtain cryptographic systems from overseas. So security professionals in the U.S. thus face a dilemma; either recommend foreign suppliers, because that is best for the client, or risk liability and due diligence claims by recommending "buy American." The effect on Internet commerce, one of the attractions of which is its global reach, is to produce a lowest common denominator effect in terms of cryptographic strength.[11] This undermines user confidence, although the rate at which current codes are being rendered obsolete by improvements in affordable, computer-based cracking techniques is hopefully slower than the rate at which Washington is changing its tune on these issues.

In terms of government restrictions on cryptography, we have seen one company, Trusted Information Systems, the firewall vendor, obtain an export license for encryption which does not require escrowing with a government agency.[12] Hopefully, this is an indication that the government is going to be more business-friendly on these issues. In the following sections I review developments in the three areas of Internet commerce.

Credit Card Orders. Right now, encrypted credit card orders can be taken over the Web right by means of the Secure Sockets Layer, supported by the most widely used Web browser, NetScape Navigator, when interacting with NetScape Commerce Server, the secure version of the company's Web server software (SSL has also been implemented in other browsers, notably Microsoft's Internet Explorer). An icon in the browser indicates when it is interacting in encrypted mode. This also causes a noticeable slowdown in operations, which is one drawback to the system. Another drawback is that not everyone uses an SSL-capable browser or server. Also, adding SSL to a server costs around $500, which is a lot when the rest of the server software can be had for zero cost.[5]

Only an open security architecture, subject to intense testing and scrutiny . . . could serve as the basis for Internet security standards.

However, the most serious shadows over SSL have been cast by technical problems with the NetScape's implementation of security mechanisms.[13] While these are based on strong public key encryption technology, plus the RC4 private key stream cipher, from RSA (now owned by Security Dynamics), it would appear that, at times, the enormous pressure to bring products to market has triumphed over quality control. The only other explanation for some of the holes found in NetScape (such as the weak seeding of the random number generator) is that the software engineers themselves did not fully understand what they were doing. Either explanation is disconcerting for companies taking orders via the Web and consumers already hesitant to transmit their credit card information over the Internet.

There have been encouraging moves to consolidate, coordinate and publish standards. Microsoft and NetScape agreed to place their respective encryption specifications in the public domain and combine SSL 3.0 with PCT 2.0 into STLP (Secure Transport Layer Protocol, which also includes the European Secure Shell Remote Login spec). We were particularly pleased that there will be no charge for the reference and object source code versions. At the same time, the W3 and CommerceNet consortiums agreed on JEPI (Joint Electronic Payments Initiative) to cover the specifics of credit card processing.

We doubt that the Internet is stable and reliable enough yet for companies to bet on [Virtual Private Networks].

Virtual Private Networks. We doubt that the Internet is stable and reliable enough yet for companies to bet on this technology. We would hate to see people try it, get disgusted, then desert in droves. This could turn the Internet into a short-lived, proof-of-concept entity, side-lined by purely commercial, aggressively-marketed systems that capitalize upon a proven demand for secure, high-bandwidth, broad-access, computer-enabled communications. On the other hand, the constant pressure on the bottom line may lead companies which now rely on VANs for EDI to promote the Internet as a cheap alternative, forcing improvements in security and reliability (according to SKL Technology, some 64,000 companies were using EDI in 1995, but the number is expected to increase to half a million by the year 2000, with much of that growth coming from Asia and the Pacific Rim).

Digital Certificates. There has been considerable progress on SMIME, Secure Multipurpose Internet Mail Extensions. This will soon be added to products to give you the ability to sign and authenticate anything you send via email. At the same time, PGP is expanding its scope by enabling the use of trusted third parties for key holding, a more commercially attractive solution than the original web-of-trust approach.

At the same time, malicious events like the recent spoofing of news announcements suggests that we cannot assume any aspect of Internet operation will escape the attention of electronic vandals. There will be attacks on certificate holders and we must prepare for them accordingly.

The future of Internet commerce security

While the eventual emergence of security standards for Internet transactions is expected, it will not automatically result in secure Internet transactions. Even if governments relent and allow strong encryption, even if marketing departments listen to engineering and permit masterful implementations, there are a wealth of security issues that will continue to require attention:

- internal security (in all surveys to date, at least 75% of all information security infractions are by insiders and the figure is comparable or higher for credit card and commercial fraud),
- continued hacking (systems will need to evolve as hacking eats

away at current technology—the process is iterative and never-ending),

- social engineering (without proper security awareness training, organizations will continue to be susceptible to costly social engineering attacks),
- malicious code (this will continue to impose overhead on all open network systems and is likely to prosper in enhanced functionality environments such as Java and OLE, the Microsoft Internet Safe Code Initiative notwithstanding),
- reliability and performance (problems with backbones and DNS servers are common at the moment and most current dial-up PPP connections are notoriously unreliable and slow, which will probably not improve until there is widespread use of ISDN [Integrated Service Digital Network]),
- skills shortages (there are not enough people who know enough about how this technology works, a problem only made worse by the 24x7 up-time requirements of the global Internet),
- and denial of service attacks (using brute force with malice or extortion as the motive, hardware and software independent and possibly "encouraged" by improvements in confidentiality and integrity mechanisms).

In other words, the experience and wisdom of the seasoned infosec professional will continue to be of great value, and will have to be heeded if systems are to retain user/consumer confidence. Being able to think like a hacker, while acting like a guardian of the public trust, will always be a requirement for assuring the security of computer-based information. And the need to promote ethical behavior in all aspects of business and personal life will remain a priority if we are not to cripple powerful new technology with ancient human weaknesses.

Notes:

1. Not only does this FAQ contain some detailed code fixes and suggestions, it sheds a lot of light on the security issues that professionals coming to the Web from other fields sometimes find hard to appreciate. For example, why do so many Web sites use free server software? Because you get the source code, typically not available with commercial packages, and traditional Unix folks seldom trust any program the source code of which is not published.

    There is a link to the WWW Security FAQ at www.ncsa.com. Here are the main Web risks that Stein identifies: (1) Private or confidential documents stored in the Web site's document tree falling into the hands of unauthorized individuals, (2) Private or confidential information sent by the remote user to the server (such as credit card information) being intercepted, (3) Information about the Web server's host machine leaking through, giving outsiders access to data that can potentially allow them to break into the host, (4) Bugs that allow outsiders to execute commands on the server's host machine, allowing them to modify and/or damage the system. This includes "denial of service" attacks, in which the attackers pummel the machine with so many requests that it is rendered effectively useless.

And here are three truths to live by: (1) Buggy software opens security holes; (2) Complex programs always contain bugs; (3) Web servers are complex programs.

2. See the NCSA Firewall Policy Guide, which can be downloaded from www.ncsa.com.

3. For more about cypherpunks, see Stephen Levy in *Wired*, April 1996 and Stephen Cobb in *Internetwork*, May 1996: "The first thing to know about cypherpunks is that they like to crack codes . . . although they have no formal organization and most are not in it for the money. . . . Cypherpunks are a whole new dimension in code-breaking. They are part of an Internet phenomenon that I call the 'big brain factor'—the unprecedented amount of human brain power that the Internet can focus on any given subject." Cobb describes cypherpunks acting as "a cutting edge quality control mechanism . . . for pioneering Internet merchants."

4. *Infosecurity News*, January/February 1996, v7 n1, p.24.

5. About 66% of all Web sites use free server software, more than one in eight Web-servers use a free 32-bit multi-tasking operating system, running on non-proprietary hardware, 386/486/586 clones. Network Wizards, *Internet Domain Survey*, July 1995, http://www.nw.com/.

6. The Microsoft Windows File Sharing bug and the Microsoft Windows Password List Security Issue have been extensively reported and "fixes" are posted on the Microsoft Web site: www.microsoft.com.

7. See "Microsoft InfoSec Stall of Shame: the MISS Top Ten" in *Security Insider Report*, January 1995, v5 n1.

8. "Violation of ITAR still carries a maximum penalty of $1 million and 10 years in prison for criminal violation, or $500,000 and a 3-year export ban for civil violation." Steve Higgins, *PC Week*, February 8, 1993, v10 n5, p1. Note that ITAR was passed in 1943, during time of war and without public debate. Also note that the prison term is served in a very uncomfortable federal facility.

9. William Hugh Murray, Communications of the ACM, July 1992, v35 n7, p.13.

10. Bruce Schneier, *Applied Cryptography*, 2nd edition, John Wiley & Sons, 1995. While the book is freely exportable, a disk containing the source code listings from the book is not, which suggests that the National Security Agency believes foreigners can read but not type. See: http://www.qualcomm.com/people/pkarn/export/index.html. For extensive libraries on ITAR see: http://www.cygnus.com/~gnu/export.html and http://www.eff.org/crypto plus http://epic.org.

11. In 1995, French researcher and cypherpunk Damien Doligez used 120 workstations and two supercomputers to crack a single session encrypted with the 40-bit export version of RC4 in 8 days (see Ryan O. Tabibian, *PC Magazine*, October 24, 1995, v14, n18, p.29 and Stephan Somogyi, *Digital Media*, September 11, 1995, v5 n4, p.29). Since then, several others have accomplished the task with a variety of hardware. In fact, this weakness was predicted by NetScape, which faces, and is fighting, the same government restrictions on strong encryption encountered by all other American software companies. Bear in mind that the difficulty of cracking this particular algorithm increases exponentially with each additional

bit of key length. So a 41-bit key would theoretically take twice as long to crack as a 40-bit key, and so on. The U.S. government discourages the export of this sort of encryption software if the key length is greater than 40. By comparison, retail domestic versions of the NetScape browser are free to use a 128-bit key (the versions you download for free are limited to 40 bits).

12. See *NCSA NEWS*, March 1996.

13. Note that these "holes" are different from the "weakness" in RSA's RC4 stream cipher algorithm, employed by NetScape, demonstrated by Damien Doligez (see 11 above).

10

Compulsive Internet Use Could Become a Behavioral Disorder

Morris Jones

Morris Jones is the assistant editor of the Australian monthly magazine Internet Australasia.

Many computer users who access Internet chat networks, cyberspace "rooms," newsgroups, the World Wide Web, and other applications could discover that time spent on the Internet is adversely affecting their lives. Researchers warn against inordinate Internet use that reduces social or work activities. Although psychologists and other observers disagree whether compulsive Internet use is a true addiction, they acknowledge that Internet bingeing is similar to other disorders.

They say you can never have too much of a good thing, and most readers would consider the Internet to be one of the best things to appear in recent times. It informs you, it entertains you, and it keeps you in touch. Could this ever be a problem? For some people, using the Internet seems to be hazardous, and a few have even found it ruining their lives. Some analysts have been quick to label these people as 'Internet addicts', a title that suggests that the cause of this condition stalks the networks like a monster. Yet others would argue that Internet addiction is a complete myth. Does an invisible enemy really hold a susceptible minority of users in its grasp? So far, this sociological wilderness of the Net has yet to be fully explored, and studies have even been led astray by a hoax sighting of the beast. Join us now on our own safari into the realm where most researchers have yet to tread.

Sightings

The concept of Internet addiction would never have surfaced without at least some evidence. An early ancestor of Internet addiction is the general

Morris Jones, "Internet Addiction: An Invisible Enemy?" *Internet Australasia* [cited January 1997]. Reprinted by permission of *Internet Australasia* magazine, Sydney, Australia.

case of computer addiction that first began to manifest itself during the PC revolution of the eighties. Adults and children alike would become transfixed with the wonders of these devices, which offered all manner of amusements and challenges to anyone with the ability to master them. Images of bug-eyed people, fuelled by caffeine and cigarettes as they hunched over their terminals for endless hours became common in cartoons. The stereotype was fairly accurate for a small minority who would proudly wear the label of 'hacker' in its original meaning as a technological innovator instead of a computer criminal. Meanwhile, millions of others simply integrated the PC as just another part of their lives. A few cases of genuinely problematic obsessions did emerge, but computer addiction never really became a major social problem within the community.

Add networking, and the attraction becomes a lot stronger. The first cases to support the notion of Internet addiction began to emerge from universities during the late eighties, when the Internet was still largely unknown to the world in general. Anecdotal evidence would routinely emerge on campuses around the world of students who seemed to log in and do almost nothing else. In the most shocking scenarios, students would spend up to 80 hours a week plugged into the Internet. These sightings in the wild would later prompt some researchers to trawl the Internet in search of samples for study, but as with the footprints of a Yeti [an apelike creature reported to inhabit the Himalayans], not everyone is convinced that the evidence is even real.

In the most shocking scenarios, students would spend up to 80 hours a week plugged into the Internet.

Oliver Egger, a student at the Swiss Institute of Technology, went in search of potential addicts with an online behaviour questionnaire he placed on the Web. Out of a total 450 respondents, 10% considered themselves to be addicted to the Internet. Yet Egger himself admits that the figure is dubious. 'It was not based on random distribution, and we could not reach addicts who are not using the Internet any more'. In fact, the amazingly high figure quoted is a reflection of just how vaguely the condition is defined. Most people who consider themselves addicted to the Internet are merely dedicated enthusiasts, but this does not prevent some people from developing conditions that are genuinely serious. Measuring this rare condition, however, is difficult. Dr Kimberly Young, an American psychologist and founder of the Centre for Online Addiction at http://www.pitt.edu/~ksy claims that no concrete data have yet been generated in her own research. 'I would think [the number of addicts] would be very low, probably in the order of less than half a percent of users', said Grant Brecht, an Australian industrial psychologist and director of CORPsych. Nevertheless, Brecht notes that the problem has already appeared in his own consultations. John Grohol, an American psychologist, estimates that the total number of addicts ranges somewhere between 3% and 7% of the Internet's population, but no more than 1% of the general community could even be considered as addicts.

The proportion of users who have problems with staying off the Net may be very small, but when the total number of users ranges in the millions, it's easy to understand why a growing collection of horror stories has already accumulated. In the worst cases, people have had relationships and jobs terminated, and have required hospitalisation in order to cure themselves.

Defining the problem

Many psychologists refuse to take the idea of Internet addiction seriously, mainly because nobody can agree on a precise definition in the first place. Illnesses are often identified by their symptoms, even if they are not specifically defined this way. With this in mind, some researchers have at least gone as far as to generate sets of diagnostic criteria for Internet addiction. Dr Kimberly Young considers activities such as compulsively checking your email and always anticipating your next Internet session as warning signs that a user may have a problem. Other indicators to look out for include losing track of time once online and logging onto personal accounts while at work.

Storm King, an American postgraduate researcher in psychology, claims that an Internet user can be considered an addict if 'a person is suffering a personal loss, and they continue this activity despite this ongoing loss'. King claims that losses in areas such as relationships, career and health are all examples.

Some researchers have tried to relate Internet addiction to the amount of time that a user spends online, but these definitions are often dubious. System administrators, researchers and journalists who use the Internet as a normal part of their work routines are difficult to compare to the recreational user who doesn't leave his terminal. In any case, the act of simply being online doesn't translate directly into the amount of participation by the user. How many of us find it convenient to leave Netscape [a World Wide Web browser] running in the background, or have their email box open all the time? Brecht observes that some psychologists may try to label people as addicts if their online time could be identified as genuinely excessive, but another definition for Internet addiction would focus more on the framework of obsessive and compulsive disorders. 'The person would want to be spending more time doing other things, but would feel that the impulse to use the Internet would be difficult to break'.

[Ivan] Goldberg warns against giving up social, occupational or recreational activities because of Internet use.

'Obsessive and compulsive behaviour is an anxiety disorder', continues David Goldman, a Sydney-based clinical psychologist. 'If you don't actually engage in the behaviour, it raises your anxiety levels'. Goldman considers activities such as frequently checking email useful examples, but differentiates compulsive disorders from addictions on the strength of their effects. '[Addiction] is generally regarded as a qualitatively different sort of disorder', he observes. Whereas compulsions are often harmless, addictions appear when the effects become dangerous.

Users who spend endless hours actively using the Internet are often merely enthusiasts rather than addicts. The services that are available are genuinely interesting, and offer many experiences that cannot be found anywhere else. Given the fact that there are so many comparatively pointless or even harmful outlets for our spare time, Internet time is arguably one of the most enriching experiences that's accessible to the general public. According to the most recent finding of the Australian Bureau of Statistics, Australians spend an average of 108 minutes per day with the non-interactive and frequently non-interesting medium of television. Arguably, the community in general needs to spend less time in front of the tube than the terminal.

More than a joke?

Addictive behavioural patterns have been observed for all manner of activities, such as work, gambling and sex. Dr Eugene Aidman from the School of Psychology at the University of Ballarat claims that many of the symptoms displayed in non-substance addictions are almost exactly the same as those displayed by drug addicts. With this in mind, one well-publicised definition of Internet addiction is essentially a carbon copy of the classical addictive stereotype. American psychologist Dr Ivan Goldberg is well known within Internet addiction circles for assembling a list of diagnostic criteria for what he has dubbed Internet Addiction Disorder, or IAD. This disorder is manifested by three or more of the following symptoms appearing in the same 12-month period. Tolerance could appear, as defined by a need for markedly increased amounts of time on the Internet to achieve satisfaction or markedly diminished effects with continued use of the same amount of time on the Internet. Goldberg also includes withdrawal symptoms such as psychomotor agitation, anxiety, obsessive thinking about what is happening on the Internet, fantasies or dreams about the Internet, and voluntary or involuntary typing movements of the fingers. Other symptoms of IAD include distress or impairment in social functioning, using the Internet to relieve withdrawal symptoms, accessing the Internet for longer periods than was intended, and a persistent desire or unsuccessful efforts to cut down or control Internet use. Rounding off the list, Goldberg warns against giving up social, occupational or recreational activities because of Internet use, using the Internet in spite of problems and spending a great deal of time on Internet-related activities such as buying Internet-related publications! The IAD diagnostic criteria have received a great deal of attention, but one problem exists with Dr Goldberg's study. The entire thing is a fake!

Internet Addiction Disorder was created as a parody of the criteria used to diagnose psychiatric disorders, and Dr Goldberg believes that most professionals are in on the joke. 'No one who is taken seriously believes that there is such a thing as IAD', said the prankster in an email interview with *Internet Australasia*. 'Most of the psychiatrists and psychologists I know are aware that IAD is a parody, not a real disorder'.

Goldberg seems to have had a lot of fun with his addiction parody, but his diagnostic criteria underscore a serious message on the eagerness of some psychologists to slap labels on any behavioural anomaly they encounter. 'IAD is just as much a true addiction as "workaholism"', he observes. 'It is a big mistake to convert all human problem behaviours into addiction language'.

In fact, IAD is based on other diagnostic criteria for addiction that have been lifted from the Diagnostic and Statistical Manual of Mental Disorders (DSM) 4, a guidebook of diagnostic criteria that can be found in the office of most practicing psychologists around the world. This encyclopedia-style reference guide chronicles a full range of mental illnesses that practitioners may encounter, and serves as a guide for identifying them and treating them. Opinions on the value of using this book vary within the psychological community, and Dr Goldberg himself vigorously campaigned against the publication of this revised version. Suggestions that the next revision of DSM should carry a specific entry for Internet addiction are almost universally denounced. David Goldman regards DSM as little more than a starting point for diagnosis. 'I think the less amount of labelling we do with people, the better', explained Grant Brecht. 'In some cases, we need to do that because there is a particular treatment that we can give to people. Once you put a label on someone, it can tend to stick, and there can be social ramifications'. Brecht claims that DSM will not require any commentary on Internet addiction unless the community at large produces large numbers of people who display the same symptoms.

A testament to the very murky nature of Internet addiction research seems to be present in the fact that, despite his intentions, Dr Goldberg has found his parody treated as fact by many in the online world. Most Netsurfers would have no reason to doubt the statement, and some members of the profession have clearly been fooled. One psychologist interviewed by *Internet Australasia* stared in amazement when told that the diagnostic criteria were bogus, claiming that the similarities to classical addiction definitions made it seem very convincing. 'It's a shame, because it's easier to talk about this in facetious ways. You can get no shortage of jokes, but there are some genuine people who aren't doing this as a joke'.

The real lure for Internet addicts is not so much being online, but being able to use the Internet's most interactive applications.

Dr Goldberg himself has been quite surprised by the reaction his IAD stunt has received. 'When I wrote my parody of a DSM 4 diagnosis, I never had the slightest idea that it would be taken seriously. If I had to do it again, I'd never have written the original message'. Goldberg claims he regularly receives email relating to his IAD parody, and around half of his audience understands that it is a joke.

The psychologist may be repenting, but one could easily wonder if an incident that Goldberg seems to treat as nothing more than a harmless prank has really been more damaging than he would like to admit. As a part of his personal joke, Goldberg actually started a mailing list for Internet addiction at i-a-s-g@netcom.com which he claims is also a part of his parody. Unfortunately, this prank has also become involved in more serious affairs when people who claimed to be in genuine distress began to appear, assuming the list had been created in good faith. Dr Goldberg's pranks have done much to illuminate the occasionally hazy operations of psychology as a scientific discipline, but one could question if the man has breached professional and ethical guidelines in the process. Whatever the case, the joke has probably hindered the work of those who are trying to make studying the question of Internet addiction respectable, and has probably confused or misdirected thousands of people who would have read of IAD.

The real lure

The Internet holds so many uses and applications that it can be difficult to generalise about its addictive potential. Anecdotal evidence and interviews carried out by *Internet Australasia* suggest that the real lure for Internet addicts is not so much being online, but being able to use the Internet's most interactive applications. 'It is not the information available on the Internet that is so powerfully reinforcing, it is the ability to connect with one's peers, no matter where in the world they are or when those peers are able to log on', remarked Storm King.

Generally, this means that IRC (Internet Relay Chat) and MUDs (Multi-User Dungeons) have become the two principal domains for the potential addict. IRC is by far the most common feature in every tale of addiction or alleged addiction that has been documented. The reasons why this is so are varied.

One psychologist claimed that IRC offers people who may be shy or feel inadequate in normal social situations a better way to interact with the world. It allows people to only reveal as much about themselves as they want to reveal, and gives them the freedom to easily back out of any encounters they may not like. The geographical separation as well as the lack of auditory and visual cues are appealing. 'You don't have the anxiety and fear of being face to face with someone', observes Brecht, 'and you don't have to observe their reactions'. Even when a user isn't a social misfit, IRC offers people the opportunity to meet people they would never be able to encounter in real life.

If IRC offers a more attractive slant on the real world, MUDs can offer people worlds that simply cannot exist anywhere else. 'I think that MUDs are addictive due to the fact that people can interact in ways that can be impossible in real life', said Ruth Hiner, an American MUD enthusiast. 'When a person enters a MUD, they suddenly have people from all over the world greeting them and wanting to be their friend. A person normally confined to a wheelchair can do acrobatic manoeuvres on a MUD. A person who is grossly overweight can portray themselves as a sex object. You can make yourself into whatever you want to'. The ultimate arena for escapism, MUDs also allow people to engage in activities that would be forbidden in real life, and literally allow their players to get away with murder.

Together, both MUDs and IRC offer a high level of interactivity coupled with a degree of protection that is highly seductive. Yet the goal-oriented nature of MUDs seems to produce compulsions in players that can even outstrip IRC use. Hiner cites examples of people playing MUDs continuously for as long as 48 hours in an effort to achieve 'wizard' status, a highly coveted level for experienced players that gives players many privileges within the game. MUD addiction seems to be especially common amongst university students, and Hiner witnessed one case where a student's parents were forced to fly to the USA from India in order to supervise their MUD-addicted son during his final exams. Another case Hiner has personally witnessed is particularly tragic. A player who had been exploiting a bug in a MUD that gave him an unfair advantage in combat was challenged by the MUD's administrators, which produced a reaction that neither Hiner nor her colleagues had ever suspected. 'He told us that due to playing our game, he had failed all of his classes and was about to flunk out of college, and his girlfriend left him. The game was all that he had left in his life. From that day on, whenever I would see someone that would be logged on for a day or so straight, I wanted to take them aside and tell them that there's more to life than what's on a computer screen'.

Like gamblers sitting before slot machines, the potential for discovering a rich nugget of information is always present for surfers.

Grant Brecht notes that in the worst cases for IRC, people may become obsessed with a particular relationship they have formed on the Internet and may pursue it to an excessive degree. 'It's almost like Internet stalking'.

By far the most media-rich interactive environment that's currently widespread on the Net is videoconferencing, including the very popular CU-SeeMe system. American enthusiast John Becker carried out an online questionnaire on CU-SeeMe, and found that most respondents felt their use was well under control. However, Becker cites anecdotal evidence of people who have either been reprimanded at work or even fired when their usage went out of control. Despite its higher level of interactivity, CU-SeeMe has yet to generate a substantial basis of addicts. Admittedly, its usage base is much smaller, but one must surely wonder if the ability to actually see and hear people detracts from the anonymous mystique of IRC and MUDs. Internet telephony should offer an interesting compromise between not seeing a person and having some indication of their real-life characteristics, yet no report of addictive behaviour seems to have emerged for this medium.

Even when interactive applications are still not being used, the Internet's promise of instant information can still hold a degree of addictive appeal. Like gamblers sitting before slot machines, the potential for discovering a rich nugget of information is always present for surfers.

Profile of an addict

The typical stereotype of an Internet addict is fairly close to the classic image of the original computer hacker: a young male with a love of technology and poor social skills. Surveys tend to suggest that a large proportion of compulsive Internet users fit this profile, but self-styled addicts can be found from almost any background. John Becker reports that his own studies of CU-SeeMe addicts are socially isolated people at universities and research institutions, but this result is arguably just a demonstration of the sort of people who have access to the technology in the first place. Other surveys produce results that are clearly biased towards the demographic spectrum of Internet users in general. When these results are normalised, it would seem that the addictive potential is independent of any particular group.

Compulsive Internet usage isn't widespread at the present, but many analysts seem to feel that the problem will escalate.

Such a result is understandable, in light of a conclusion that has been reached by most psychologists working in this area: Internet addiction is not so much an isolated problem that flows from the Net to its victims, but the result of a deeper psychological affliction that is merely manifesting itself through Internet usage. 'I think there are a core set of psychological issues that underlie all "psychological" addictions', remarked clinical psychologist John Suler. 'Probably the most common and basic problem is a deficit in one's sense of self: a "hole" or void in one's identity, self-esteem or self worth that needs to be filled'.

One practicing psychologist encountered a direct example in his own practice. 'I saw a lawyer who came for treatment of his depression. While taking a history from him he related that in the month prior to his initial appointment with me, he had spent all day at work "surfing the Net" and that he had no billable hours. He responded well to antidepressant therapy, and as his depression improved the percentage of his work time that was spent surfing gradually decreased to zero'.

Help!

Opinions on the nature and the causes of compulsive Internet usage are varied. It's little wonder, therefore, that even professional psychologists can be divided on what people who believe they have a problem should do about it. The most common form of advice that circulates on the Net itself is to simply cut back on usage. 'They should introduce impulse control, and switch the thing off', advises Grant Brecht. 'They need to develop a habit of doing this, and plan their Net time each day. It's like breaking any form of negative addiction. If they find relationships are suffering or they are spending more time or money than they like, see a psychologist for a few sessions'.

It's worth noting that most Web sites with titles that suggest they are help centres for Internet addicts are usually parodies, and certain newsgroups that seem to be targeted at addicts seem to have nothing in them that's on-topic. John Grohol bluntly states that 'joining an online support group is contra-indicated'. Indeed, there seems to be little hope of reduc ing a person's Internet time by using it as treatment!

David Goldman sees no point in offering advice to addicts at all. 'A person is not going to respond to any kind of help if they don't feel like tackling the problem and are perfectly happy with what most of us would call an addiction. If they are forced to seek help by a third party, the efficacy of treatment is pretty minimal'.

In reality, evidence suggests that most users with serious clinical conditions will either be unaware that they may have a problem, or will be unprepared to admit it. Maressa Hecht Orzack, the founder of one of the world's very small handful of computer addiction centres at McLean Hospital in the USA notes that 'the level of denial is so strong that we have more referrals from families than from addicted individuals themselves'. Patients who pass through her program range from homesick students who are failing courses because of their Internet usage to patients suffering from the under-reported condition of information overload.

Too much!

If some users spend excessive amounts of time on the Internet because they want to, a growing number are doing so because they feel they have to. A survey of business managers around the world released by Reuters Business Information suggests that information overload is more than just a catchy phrase. According to Diccon Close from Reuters, 100 Australian managers were confidentially polled during 1996, with results that suggested that information overload and a compulsive need to access it were causing serious problems. 'It was a surprise to find that people were not as well prepared as they thought they would be, and are even showing signs of ill health'. In fact, Australians seem to be suffering more than their international counterparts. 'Sixty-nine percent of Australian managers, compared to 62% of managers worldwide, testify that their personal relationships suffer due to information overload. Sixty-two percent are also believed to suffer ill health, compared to 52% globally'. Close remarks that 27% of Australian managers believe that the Internet has contributed to the accumulation of information, but are confused by its poor organisational structure. 'For business information, it's like wandering into a library with the lights off, knowing that a book you want is in there somewhere'.

The next generation

Compulsive Internet usage isn't widespread at the present, but many analysts seem to feel that the problem will escalate as a new generation is raised with online services from their earliest years. 'Children become very proficient in the use of technological devices in Primary School, including the Internet', remarks Grant Brecht. 'The fascination with that could really absorb a great deal of time, especially with children who are socially shy. They could feel safer on the Internet than mixing with other children. It will probably only affect a few vulnerable individuals, but the Internet may aid in producing a disorder'. Some users are already monitoring the amount of time spent by children online, but the 'technology gap' between the generations means that some parents are simply unaware of how much time their family is spending online. Using the Internet as a baby sitter is tempting, but could be detrimental if it is used at the expense of normal social interactions.

Other researchers simply believe that once the world's fascination with the Internet as a novelty ends, interest in Internet addiction will simply fade. The problem itself could also disappear as people become both familiar and comfortable with the technology. Ultimately, it is the users who will decide how the Internet will fit into the greater matrix of life, and the choice will be up to everyone individually.

11

Copyright Infringement
May Increase on the Internet

The Economist

The Economist *is a British weekly magazine covering international affairs.*

Intellectual property—including art, databases, music, and software—is increasingly the target of copyright infringement. Copyright owners are losing much money as their property is pirated from the Internet, copied, and illegally sold. Copyright infringement is likely to increase as digital technology and the Internet grow and make it easy to copy or alter many forms of intellectual property. Efforts by producers and exporters to increase copyright protection will likely diminish private citizens' access to free information.

"The Internet is one gigantic copying machine," says David Nimmer, a Los Angeles lawyer who spends his time advising owners of intellectual property on their rights to their evanescent assets. "All copyrighted works can now be digitised, and once on the Net, copying is effortless, costless, widespread and immediate."

For lots of the rich world's most successful industries, that is dire news. Intellectual property is big business. Many modern products sell, not for what the physical object costs to make, but for a price that reflects heavy research costs (think of drugs) or an ingenious idea (software) or spending on branding (perfume). High development costs, coupled with low production costs, make such products vulnerable to piracy. The low cost of each extra fake means that consumer and pirate share an interest in diddling the original investor.

In the past, copying intellectual products has been time-consuming and the reproduction sometimes worse than the original. But digital technology changes things in two main ways. First, the quality of copies is as good as the master. The difference between a fake Michael Jackson CD and the real thing is much smaller than that between a pirated audio cassette and the genuine article. Second, the border-disregarding Internet

"The Property of the Mind," *Economist*, July 27, 1996. Copyright ©1996, The Economist, Ltd. Distributed by, and reprinted by permission of, New York Times Special Features/Syndication Sales.

makes it easy to deliver works to a vast number of people.

Once copyright works are widely distributed over the Internet, the conspiratorial interests of the pirate and the consumer blend seamlessly together. For any individual can, in theory, copy or alter any digitised work and distribute it at a few keystrokes to hundreds of friends. The new world that faces content industries is one in which the pirate and the potential customer may often be the same person.

Every year, the Business Software Alliance (BSA) compares sales of computers with sales of software. Working on a rule of thumb that a PC uses an average of almost three packages—a word-processor, a spreadsheet, and perhaps one other—it reckons that at least half the global market is supplied by pirated products. The International Federation of the Phonographic Industry (IFPI) reckons that one in five sales of recorded music is of a pirated copy. In the case of CDs, one in three sales by value is pirated.

Piracy figures that purport to show lost sales, as opposed to pirated copies as a proportion of total sales, are often overestimates. Many of those who buy fake software would never have paid the full price. Some defend piracy as a form of promotion, arguing that a generation of young Chinese has now grown used to (fake) Microsoft software. Neither argument disguises the fact that the "lost" market is huge, and the digital age will expand it.

One reason is that it will expand enormously what might be called the market for "altruistic" piracy. Many unauthorised copies, especially of software and music, are not sold by organised gangs but given away by people who do not think of it as a crime. PolyGram, a large Dutch recording company, reckons that three times as much music is privately copied as is legally sold. This article will probably be photocopied and passed around the offices of exactly the same organisations that queue up to denounce copyright theft.

This means that the content providers face a political challenge as well as a practical one: to convince people that stealing a piece of information is theft just like stealing a car. As Thomas Jefferson pointed out, somebody could take his idea and still leave him with what he originally had: "as he who lights his taper at mine receives light without darkening me." Many Internet fanatics like that attitude. But in Jefferson's day, legal copyright protection was young (the first statute was passed in Britain in 1709); and Americans, as Britain's authors endlessly complained, were notorious for pirating other countries' publications. Now that the United States is the world's biggest exporter of intellectual property, its politicians think differently.

The force of law

A report by Price Waterhouse, a consultancy, points to a scene depicting the 1963 March on Washington in that triumph of digital inventiveness, *Forrest Gump*. It was filmed by taking a small group of actors, and digitally multiplying them into a crowd. Stored away for future use, the clip could be turned into a 1990s crowd scene with a few digitised haircuts. Who owns the rights: the original filmers, or the technician who transformed their work?

West Hills Community College District
Fitch Library
Coalinga Campus
Coalinga CA 93210

The point about this example is that, even when piracy is not involved, digital formats pose copyright conundrums. Even knottier problems arise once copyright material gets anywhere near the Internet. Copyright law confers two main rights: to authorise reproduction (ie, the making of copies), and to authorise the distribution of those copies. "The most basic question", says William Tanenbaum, a lawyer with Rogers & Wells in New York, "is the nature of electronic transmission of a copyright work: is it reproduction or distribution or both?"

So far, nobody knows. Indeed, the digital age poses problems for traditional notions of both "reproduction" and "distribution".

Copyright law currently makes a distinction between reproduction for public use (which can be done only with the rights-holder's permission) and private use (which, within certain limits, is sometimes allowed to give users reasonable access to small bits of information). For instance, most publishers are happy for libraries to allow books to be copied by readers. However, now that everyone can download a perfect copy of a whole database or a video clip, should that distinction be allowed?

If a surfer calls up a page of information from the Internet on to a screen, is that reproduction? After all, if the information is held merely in the computer's RAM, or short-term memory, it will vanish if the user switches off. But lawyers now argue that it does infringe copyright. Mr Nimmer points out that "the RAM can hold a work for a period of more than transitory duration, and that work can be held simultaneously in the RAMs of 1,000 computers."

Most people (and national laws) think of copyright in terms of an artistic or intellectual creation. A collection of addresses or credit ratings is hardly artistic, and yet it may cost a lot to compile. Do databases deserve a special, copyright-type protection?

Under most copyright law, the distribution right controls the first sale of a copy, but not subsequent sales (so, for instance, a student can freely sell a second-hand textbook). But what if the initial copy can be perfectly copied again and again? "In a digital world", says Mark Turner of Garrett, a London firm of solicitors, "the key question is what copying is allowed."

Current copyright law is based around national boundaries. The right to distribute copies of a CD or magazine in one country does not allow those copies to be sold in another. Many content importers, especially developing countries, say this territorial restriction thwarts trade; America and Europe understandably want it to stay.

A harsher world

Many expert groups are beavering away on new rules to deal with these points. In the United States, a group chaired by Bruce Lehman, the assistant commerce secretary, has drawn up proposals to revise copyright law. In the European Union, another group in 1995 drew up a green (consultative) paper on "copyright and related rights in a digital society", which may eventually become a directive. And the World Intellectual Property Organisation, a United Nations body based in Geneva, is trying to update the elderly Berne Convention which sets international standards for copyright laws.

In general the content producers and exporters involved in these groups are likely to take a tough theoretical stand, and try to extend copyright protection to new sorts of intellectual property. For instance, a European directive extends copyright protection to databases. In particular, they are likely to argue that almost any kind of electronic reproduction or distribution of a copyright work requires the permission of the owner.

Even when piracy is not involved, digital formats pose copyright conundrums. Even knottier problems arise once copyright material gets anywhere near the Internet.

This means that the rights to free information that private citizens had in a pre-digital world will almost inevitably be diminished. Libraries will be an early target. Eric Gahrau of Bertelsmann, a giant German media conglomerate, deplores the holes in German law: "It's a complete catastrophe: vast exceptions for private copying allow a library to make a legal copy of a publication for its archives, and then to transmit it."

But what of the consequences of shutting such loopholes? Pamela Samuelson, professor of law at the University of California in Berkeley, argues that "people have a strong sense that what they do in their own home is nobody else's business; but the public's perception, and that of many publishers, is getting further and further apart."

Pay me

Suppose that copyright provisions are tightened up. Can they be made to work? Clive Bradley of Britain's Publishers Association argues that it will become essential to have a payments system that can charge users of intellectual property for what they use: for the information in a database that is actually used, rather than for the database itself.

But it will be immensely difficult. Part of the problem will be to monitor when copyright material is being used. That requires, in the first place, some way of identifying the owner of a right. Books have an internationally agreed numbering system, but it identifies only the physical volume and not its contents. Several competing schemes are being designed to identify the owners of other sorts of rights. Imprimatur, an organisation financed by the European Commission, is trying to keep track of such schemes, in the hope that common international standards will develop.

That is all very laudable, but the difficulties are huge. Not until 1995, says Chris Barlas, who runs the Imprimatur project, was there an internationally accepted system to identify films and television programmes. Even with an agreed numbering system, there has to be some way to attach an identifying sign, or watermark, to every copyrighted work. Such a sign has to appear on fragments of a work: a few bars of music, say, or a couple of stills from a film. Thorn EMI, a British music company, claims to have come up with a system that will work for music recordings.

Once a trade in rights can be identified, how should it be billed? Ideally, perhaps, every time somebody visited an Internet site that used a particular picture, the artist would receive a tiny payment; every time somebody looked at a page of a guidebook, the viewer would be billed a fragment of a penny. But this would require such a complex billing system that its cost might well exceed the revenue it produced.

Producers whose works combine several sorts of media—such as CD-ROMs—increasingly complain that conventional systems of clearing and paying for rights are cumbersome and expensive. They may have to contact different agencies for the rights to films, text and music. Worse, tariffs are linked to the number of copies that are made. In the case of new media, that is anachronistic: should the producer of a game pay an identical fee for a piece of music played right at the start, which every user will hear, and for a tune played only at level ten, which only the best players will enjoy?

Solving and simplifying payments problems is an essential part of persuading people to stick to the rules of copyright use. For if paying for something is easy and reasonable, people are much more likely to be law-abiding than if it is complicated and expensive.

The thought police

How is copyright infringement to be curtailed? Content producers see three options: technology, law enforcement and public education. As a rule, the more low-tech an industry, the greater its faith in technological answers and vice versa. Charles Clark, of the Federation of European Publishers, likes to intone that "the answer to the machine is in the machine."

Certainly a huge technological effort is being made to develop pirate-proof ways to transmit material. For example, IBM has developed a system of secure "packaging" for sending digital information over the Internet, and a clearing house through which commercial content providers can track delivery of and payment for contents held in such "packages". But most software companies are pessimistic. Ron Barker of [network software manufacturer] Novell, which claims to lose $1 billion a year to the pirates, says gloomily: "Every time somebody comes up with a new technology, it takes just a week or two to get around it."

Part of the problem will be to monitor when copyright material is being used.

Companies such as Novell would prefer governments to clamp down on piracy. Thanks to the agreement on trade-related aspects of intellectual property rights (TRIPS), governments have to incorporate international copyright agreements such as the Berne Convention into national law. But laws need to be enforced. The BSA's Allen Dixon argues that a campaign in Italy has helped to reduce pirating of software from 90% in 1990 to 57% in 1994. "Even if you bring piracy rates down from 90% to 80%," he says, "you have doubled the size of the market." This strategy is fine as long as most pirates are businesses. But no government is likely to send the police to bash down doors at dawn in search of bootlegging by private citizens for their own use.

The Internet helps the enforcers in one way. Piracy is easy to spot. Just type into one of the many search services a couple of sentences of a story from the *Economist*, and you will be able to discover any pirated version of the piece. Sometimes, it can then be quickly rooted out. In April 1995, a group of Norwegian students loaded several hundred music albums on to the Internet, using a server at their university, and offered them free of charge. The IFPI in Norway contacted their university and the site was shut down.

More often, cases are like that of Magicom, a German company selling thousands of bootlegged recordings through mail order, advertising them on the Internet. When their British Internet service provider was threatened with legal action, the page was withdrawn from the Net—but is now back, using a service provider based in Luxembourg. Luxembourg has so far failed to introduce laws to comply with either EU copyright directives or the TRIPS provisions.

Intellectual property's troubled encounter with the digital age is producing many more questions than answers.

For enforcers, the Internet creates at least two problems. First, says James Lowe, Microsoft's head pirate-chaser, it may be hard to track down the source of illicit material. People put it on to the Net anonymously: "There's a hacker mentality in cyberspace." The server on which pirated "warez" (sic) are held may be in one country, the server through which they are advertised in another, the seller in a third.

Second, once tracked, it may be hard to decide who is liable. One American court case (involving an infringement of *Playboy* magazine's copyright in some photographs) found the operator of the bulletin board that displayed them liable, even though he did not know of his subscribers' actions. Another, involving extracts from publications by the Church of Scientology, has reached the opposite view. Different countries will, in time, probably take different views of liability.

That creates scope for another problem: the evolution of copyright havens, where professional pirates will set up servers from which they can sell pirated wares. Garrett's Mr Turner claims to know of a large telecoms company which has been approached by a company wanting to set up an offshore base to sell bootlegged data.

Will these headaches drive content companies out of business? Probably not, although they may destroy some of their profits. For one thing, however ingenious hackers may be, it will take a certain amount of time and ingenuity for the mass of ordinary people to benefit from their skills. Companies will face a trade-off: the higher the profit margin on their products, the greater the incentive for ordinary folk to crack encryption systems and buy from Luxembourg pirates.

After all, Hollywood has survived for years even though television companies broadcast its films (admittedly months after their initial release). Most people trade off the bother of wrestling with the video recorder against the low cost of renting the same film from the nearest store.

One answer to pirating is to make the real thing more valuable than the bootleg. Frequent updates may do that: not many people will bother to pirate a financial newsletter that is updated every day, or even every hour. Another answer, put forward (in a pricey newsletter) by Esther Dyson, an American cyber-guru, is for content providers to look for other ways to make money from their intellectual property. For instance, a company could give away its CD, but try to raise money from advertising or sponsorship. Or it can charge for spin-offs: the Grateful Dead, a pop group, long allowed people to record its concerts, and made money from the admission tickets.

This vision appeals to many Net folk. But there are doubts about its practicability. It might be fine for an entertaining speaker to give away his books, and hope to make the money back from seminars; but it is far harder for obscure authors. Netscape, a successful Internet firm, began by giving its Web browser away for free; now it charges $50 a shot. For the moment, at least, intellectual property's troubled encounter with the digital age is producing many more questions than answers.

12

The Internet Is Collapsing

Bob Metcalfe

Bob Metcalfe invented Ethernet, a network operating system, in 1973 and founded 3Com Corporation, a San Francisco computer hardware manufacturer, in 1979. He writes the "From the Ether" column for InfoWorld, a weekly magazine covering computers and the Internet.

The Internet is headed for a catastrophic collapse. Internet congestion and prolonged service outages are signs of this impending failure. Other weak spots include software bugs, human error, and sabotage. Many corporations and universities recognize the potential for collapse and have created their own "intranets"—private networks for selected users. Internet service providers and Internet management organizations should seek solutions to improve Internet performance.

The Internet might possibly escape a "gigalapse" in 1996. If so, I'll be eating columns at the World Wide Web Conference in April 1997. Even so, Scott Bradner [a director of network management for the Internet Engineering Task Force] should still be concerned about the Internet's coming catastrophic collapses.

Collapses are widespread and prolonged Internet outages, when catastrophic enough, get named and tracked much like tropical storms.

To size an outage, multiply the number of users times their hours of denied access. A BBN Corp. "kilolapse" lost thousands of user hours. An ampersand mistyped into a router deNetted 400,000 Netcom users for 13 hours—a 5.2 "megalapse." Another botched router update deWebbed 6.2 million America Online users for 19 hours—a catastrophic 118 megalapse.

Now don't you be confusing megalapses with the Internet's bogging down. Members of the World Wide Wait Watchers Club do this. They complain about waiting too long for downloads, too often hitting their stop-loading buttons, and too seldom getting better service by changing Internet service providers (ISPs). To them, the bogging down and collapses are the same thing—a pain.

To work around the bogging and collapsing Internet, many have been building intranets. Even the universities that built the Internet are angling for their very own private new one. When will our thousands of

Bob Metcalfe, "The Internet Is Collapsing; the Question Is Who's Going to Be Caught in the Fall," *InfoWorld*, November 18, 1996. Reprinted by permission.

106

uncooperative ISPs, who count on luring users from their collapsing competitors, learn why airlines don't compete by claiming their airplanes crash less?

Among the causes of Internet collapse are traffic jams. Of course, this automobile analogy forgets that when Internet bridges are gridlocked, packets (unlike cars) get dumped into the river. The 10 percent packet losses that caught my attention in December 1995 now sometimes exceed 40 percent.

Large portions of the Internet might be brought down not by nuclear war but by power failures, telephone outages, . . . and sabotage.

Internet retransmission protocols, as widely implemented, multiply packet losses, slow downloads, and often sneak away leaving inexplicable error messages. There's a danger of regenerative retransmission collapse.

Overbuilding the Internet to overcome its architectural problems is decreasingly an option. Financial incentives for adding capacity are weak—ISPs struggle to make money. Despite all that dark fiber, actual circuits are harder to come by. Installation delays on 45Mbps [megabytes per second] backbone circuits, for example, are now stretching out toward 180 days.

Weak spots and a lack of management

Let's be concerned that large portions of the Internet might be brought down not by nuclear war but by power failures, telephone outages, overloaded domain name servers, bugs in stressed router software, human errors in maintaining routing tables, and sabotage, to name a few weak spots.

Because the Internet's builders believed that it defies management—it's alive, they say—they punted, leaving no organized process for managing Internet operations. Where are circuits inventoried, traffic forecasts consolidated, outages reported, upgrades analyzed and coordinated? As my programming friends would say, the Internet Engineering and Planning Group and the North American Network Operators' Group are by most accounts no-ops—they exist, but they don't do anything.

But the Internet is not alive. It's actually a network of computers. And somebody, hopefully cooperating ISPs, should be managing its operations.

The Internet Engineering Task Force now seems to be coming around. It reorganized itself to create an Operations and Management (O&M) Area. Scott Bradner should be re-elected to lead O&M and to organize ISP processes for cooperative operational management.

Now, some say I'm a control freak, and we should let competition in the free market save us from Internet catastrophe. Excuse me, but pundits whining their concerns, buyers getting informed, and competing service providers better organizing their cooperations are all good examples of exactly how this free market thing actually works. If we get ISPs cooperating on operations soon, maybe our growing governments and their telephone monopolies won't need to step in to save the Internet's day.

Glossary

ARPANET   One of the world's first computer networks, now defunct, created by the Department of Defense's Advanced Research Projects Agency in the 1970s.

bandwidth   A section of the electromagnetic **spectrum** occupied by some form of signal, e.g., data, fax, television, voice, etc. Signals require a certain size and location of bandwidth in order to be transmitted. The higher the frequency of the bandwidth, the faster the signal transmission, thus allowing for more complex signals, such as audio or video, to be transmitted. Because bandwidth is a limited space, heavy demand often forces users to wait their turn. Bombarding the **Internet** with unnecessary information is referred to as "taking up bandwidth."

browser   A software tool used to read electronic documents. Mosaic, NetScape, and Lynx are popular browsers.

Communications Decency Act (CDA)   A 1996 law, also known as the Exon Amendment, that banned the availability to minors of indecent material on the **Internet**.

cyberspace   The nebulous "place" where humans interact over computer networks (the **Internet** is considered cyberspace). Coined by author William Gibson in his 1984 science fiction novel *Neuromancer*.

download   To receive a file or program from another computer.

e-mail   Electronic mail sent via a computer network.

encryption   A type of software that encodes computer users' communications in order to protect their privacy. The U.S. government has forbidden the exportation of encryption software, such as Pretty Good Privacy (PGP).

Ethernet   A network operating system.

FAQs   Frequently Asked Questions. A collection of information describing the basics of many computer-related subjects. Often put together and archived on a **server** so that computer users do not unnecessarily take up **bandwidth** by asking simple questions.

fiber optics   A high-speed data transmission channel made of high-purity glass strands sealed within an opaque tube. Because it uses light as a carrier wave, transmission via fiber optics is much faster and more powerful than via metal wire channels such as coaxial cable.

flame   To post an insulting message against another **Internet** user.

Free-Nets   Local organizations that offer **Internet** access to the public at no cost.

FTP   File Transfer Protocol. A standard used to transfer one computer's data to another computer, such as in **downloading** or **uploading**, or the program used to transfer the data.

HTML **Hypertext** Markup Language. A convention of codes that makes information accessible on the **World Wide Web**. HTML codes allow Web **browsers** to read such information.

hypertext A document that has been designed to allow a user to select words or pictures within the document and to connect to related information. It provides the basis for the **World Wide Web**.

Information Superhighway A catchphrase used to describe the growing system of universal, internetworked communications services. Officially known as the National Information Infrastructure (**NII**).

Internet The largest international computer network, made up of scores of smaller networks linked together by international **protocols**.

intranet A private network accessed only by selected users.

IP **Internet Protocol**. The international standard for addressing and transmitting data on the **Internet**.

IRC **Internet** Relay Chat. An on-line group discussion.

ISDN Integrated Services Digital Network. A service that sends digital signals over telephone lines much faster than standard telephone transmissions. It requires special hardware and software.

listserv An **e-mail** program that allows multiple computer users to connect to a single system, thus creating an on-line discussion. The **Internet** contains thousands of listservs on various subjects.

Luddites Persons opposed to technological change.

modem From modulator/demodulator. The commonly used hardware that is used to connect personal computers to distant computers or networks.

MOO **MUD** Object Oriented. Alternatives to **MUDs**, MOOs are collections of virtual spaces, or "rooms," created by computer users in which participants can construct and manipulate objects and interact with each other.

MUD Multiple User Domain or Multiple User Dungeon. Frequently used for games, MUDs are fixed virtual environments designed by programmers that allow computer users to congregate, interact, and move from one space to another.

multimedia Any document that uses multiple forms of communication, such as text, audio, and/or video.

NII National Information Infrastructure. The growing communications network that will interconnect much of society. It is commonly referred to as the **Information Superhighway**.

PCS Personal Communication Services. A broad range of radio communication services for personal use, including wireless faxes, paging systems, etc.

PDA Personal Digital Assistant. A handheld electronic device that stores text and graphics in memory.

Postscript files A printing format used by many computer printers.

PPP Point-to-Point Protocol. A software package that gives users direct telephone connections to the **Internet**. PPP is quickly replacing an older standard known as **SLIP**.

protocol   A definition or standard designed to allow different computers and different networks to communicate internationally.

RSA   RSA Data Security Inc. A company specializing in **encryption** and authentication software.

server   A computer or program that allows other computers to access information stored on it.

SLIP   Serial Line **Internet Protocol**. It allows a user to connect to the **Internet** directly over a high-speed **modem**.

spam   To send unwanted messages to **Internet** users.

spectrum   The range of electromagnetic frequencies used for all forms of transmission.

TCP   Transmission Control Protocol (also known as **IP/TCP**). A **protocol** that ensures that packets of data are shipped and received in their intended order.

upload   To send a file or program to another computer.

USENET   A "newsgroup," or discussion group, that is accessed via the **Internet**.

World Wide Web   Also known as WWW, W3, or the Web. A collection of thousands of "websites" on the **Internet** devoted to specific companies, governments, individuals, organizations, and schools.

Organizations to Contact

The editors have compiled the following list of organizations concerned with the issues debated in this book. The descriptions are derived from materials provided by the organizations themselves. All have publications or information available for interested readers. The list was compiled on the date of publication of the present volume; names, addresses, phone and fax numbers, and e-mail/Internet addresses may change. Be aware that many organizations take several weeks or longer to respond to inquiries, so allow as much time as possible.

Center for Democracy and Technology (CDT)
1634 I St. NW, Suite 1100
Washington, DC 20006
(202) 637-9800
fax: (202) 637-0968
e-mail: info@cdt.org
Internet: http://www.cdt.org

CDT is a public-interest organization supported by individuals, foundations, and a broad cross section of the computer and communications industries. The center's mission is to develop public policies that preserve and advance democratic values and constitutional civil liberties on the Internet and in other interactive communications media. It offers information via its website.

Center for Media Education (CME)

1511 K St. NW, Suite 518
Washington, DC 20005
(202) 628-2620
fax: (202) 628 2554
e-mail: cme@access.digex.net
Internet: http://www.cme.org/cme

CME is concerned with media and telecommunications issues, such as educational television for children, universal public access to the information highway, and the development and ownership of information services. It is involved in several projects, including the Campaign for Kids TV, which seeks to improve children's education. CME publishes the monthly newsletter *InfoActive: Telecommunications Monthly for Nonprofits*.

Electronic Frontier Foundation (EFF)
PO Box 170190
San Francisco, CA 94117-0190
(415) 668-7171
fax: (415) 668-7007
e-mail: eff@eff.org
Internet: http//www.eff.org

EFF is an organization of students and other individuals that aims to promote a better understanding of telecommunications issues. It fosters awareness of civil liberties issues arising from advances in computer-based communications media and supports litigation to preserve, protect, and extend First Amendment rights in computing and telecommunications technologies. EFF's publications include *Building the Open Road, Crime and Puzzlement,* the quarterly newsletter *Networks and Policy,* the biweekly electronic newsletter *EFFector Online,* as well as on-line bulletins and publications, such as *First Amendment in Cyberspace.*

Electronic Privacy Information Center (EPIC)
666 Pennsylvania Ave. SE, Suite 301
Washington, DC 20003
(202) 544-9240
fax: (202) 547-5482
e-mail: info@epic.org
Internet: http://www.epic.org

EPIC advocates a public right to electronic privacy. It sponsors educational and research programs, compiles statistics, and conducts litigation. EPIC's publications include the biweekly electronic newsletter *EPIC Alert* and on-line reports.

Interactive Services Association (ISA)
8403 Colesville Rd., Suite 865
Silver Spring, MD 20910
(301) 495-4955
e-mail: isa@aol.com
Internet: http://www.isa.com

ISA is a trade association representing more than three hundred companies in advertising, broadcasting, and other areas involving the delivery of telecommunications-based services. It has six councils, including Interactive Marketing and Interactive Television, covering the interactive media industry. The association publishes the brochure *Child Safety on the Information Superhighway,* the handbook *Gateway 2000,* the monthly newsletter *ISA Update* (delivered by fax or by e-mail), and various reports.

Internet Society
12020 Sunrise Valley Dr., Suite 210
Reston, VA 22091-3429
(703) 648-9888
(800) 468-9507
fax: (703) 648-9887
e-mail: isoc@isoc.org
Internet: http://www.isoc.org

A group of technologists, developers, educators, researchers, government representatives, and businesspeople, the Internet Society supports the development and dissemination of standards for the Internet and works to ensure global cooperation and coordination for the Internet and related Internetworking technologies and applications. It publishes the bimonthly magazine *On the Internet.*

National Computer Security Association (NCSA)
1200 Walnut Bottom Rd., Suite 3
Carlisle, PA 17013-7635
(717) 258-1816
(800) 488-4595
fax: (717) 243-8642
Internet: http://www.ncsa.com

NCSA is an organization that offers information and opinions on computer security issues. It strives to improve computer security by disseminating information and certifying security products. The association publishes the bimonthly *NCSA Newsletter.*

SafeSurf
16032 Sherman Way, Suite 58
Van Nuys, CA 91406
(818) 902-9390
fax: (818) 902-1928
e-mail: safesurf@safesurf.com
Internet: http://www.safesurf.com

The goal of SafeSurf is to prevent children from accessing adult material—including pornography—on the Internet. It maintains that standards must be implemented on the Internet to protect children. SafeSurf reviews entertainment products such as children's computer games and awards a seal of excellence to exceptional products. The organization publishes the quarterly newsletter *SafeSurf News.*

United Federation of ChildSafe Web Sites (UFCWS)
417 E. Port Hueneme Rd., Suite 120
Port Hueneme, CA 93041-3343
(805) 981-1280
fax: (805) 981-1210
e-mail: madmonk@childsafe.com
Internet: http://www.childsafe.com

The federation advocates responsible free speech and strives to make the World Wide Web a more inoffensive and enjoyable medium for children. UFCWS developed the Internet ChildSafe Certification Standard to guarantee parents that their children are accessing positive and productive Web content. It publishes the monthly electronic publication *Positive Image* and updates an electronic newsletter daily, both of which can be accessed on their Web site.

Bibliography

Books

James Boyle	*Shamans, Software, and Spleens: Law and the Construction of the Information Society.* Cambridge, MA: Harvard University Press, 1996.
John Brockman	*Digerati: Encounters with the Cyber Elite.* Emeryville, CA: Publishers Group West, 1996.
Daniel Burstein and David Kline	*Road Warriors: Dreams and Nightmares Along the Information Highway.* New York: Dutton, 1995.
Frederick B. Cohen	*Protection and Security on the Information Superhighway.* New York: Wiley, 1995.
Jim Cummins and Dennis Sayers	*Brave New Schools: Challenging Cultural Illiteracy Through Global Learning Networks.* New York: St. Martin's, 1995.
Bill Gates	*The Road Ahead.* New York: Viking, 1995.
Matthew Lyon and Katie Hafner	*Where Wizards Stay Up Late: The Origins of the Internet.* New York: Simon & Schuster, 1996.
Steven E. Miller	*Civilizing Cyberspace: Policy, Power, and the Information Superhighway.* New York: ACM Press, 1996.
Nicholas Negroponte	*Being Digital.* New York: Knopf, 1995.
O'Reilly & Associates, eds.	*Internet and Society.* Cambridge, MA: Harvard University Press, 1997.
Charles Platt	*Anarchy Online.* New York: HarperCollins, 1997.
Winn Schwartau	*Information Warfare: Chaos on the Electronic Superhighway.* New York: Thunder's Mouth Press, 1994.
Clifford Stoll	*Silicon Snake Oil: Second Thoughts on the Information Highway.* New York: Doubleday, 1995.
Steven L. Talbott	*The Future Does Not Compute: Transcending the Machines in Our Midst.* Sebastopol, CA: O'Reilly & Associates, 1995.
Don Tapscott and Ann Cavoukian	*Who Knows: Safeguarding Your Privacy in a Networked World.* New York: McGraw-Hill, 1997.
Jonathan Wallace and Mark Mangan	*Sex, Laws, and Cyber-Space: Freedom and Censorship on the Frontiers of the Online Revolution.* New York: Henry Holt, 1996.
Brad Wieners and David Pescovitz	*Reality Check.* Emeryville, CA: Publishers Group West, 1996.

Periodicals

Marcelo Alonso — "Infotech: Boon or Curse?" *World & I*, May 1996. Available from 3600 New York Ave. NE, Washington, DC 20002.

A. Armstrong and J. Hagel — "The Real Value of On-line Communities," *Harvard Business Review*, May/June 1996.

John Perry Barlow — "A New Declaration: The Independence of Cyberspace," *Rights*, April/June 1996.

Frank Beacham — "Net Loss," *Extra!* May/June 1996.

Solveig Bernstein — "Beyond the Communications Decency Act: Constitutional Lessons of the Internet," *Cato Policy Analysis*, November 4, 1996.

S.A. Booth — "Essential Technology Guide: Education," *Popular Science*, September 1996.

Cato Policy Report — "The Future of Money in the Information Age," July/August 1996. Available from the Cato Institute, 1000 Massachusetts Ave. NW, Washington, DC 20001.

CQ Researcher — "Clashing over Copyright: Is the Intellectual Property Safe in the Internet Age?" vol. 6, no. 42, November 8, 1996. Available from Congressional Quarterly Inc., 1414 22nd St. NW, Washington, DC 20037.

Tom Dowe — "News You Can Abuse," *Wired*, January 1997. Available from 520 Third St., 4th Fl., San Francisco, CA 94107.

Mark Draper — "Beyond Cyberspace: The Real Promise of Virtual Reality," *Vital Speeches of the Day*, September 15, 1995.

Fortune — Special section: "Why the Net Means Business," December 9, 1996.

Freedom — Special issue: "Freedom of Speech at Risk in Cyberspace," vol. 28, no. 1, 1995. Available from Church of Scientology International, 6331 Hollywood Blvd., Suite 1200, Los Angeles, CA 90028-6329.

David Gelernter — "Inter-Not," *Utne Reader*, November/December 1996.

William Gibson — "The Net Is a Waste of Time. And That's Exactly What's Right About It," *New York Times Magazine*, July 14, 1996.

Douglas Gomery — "The Future of Computer Communications: Centralized or Decentralized—Which World Will the Internet Bring?" *American Enterprise*, March/April 1996.

Andrew S. Grove — "Is the Internet Overhyped?" *Forbes*, September 23, 1996.

Steven Levy — "Breathing Is Also Addictive," *Newsweek*, December 30, 1996–January 6, 1997.

Peter H. Lewis — "Technology: Talk of Internet's Collapse Greatly Exaggerated," *New York Times Magazine*, September 2, 1996.

Scott Marshall	"The Internet, the Future, and Who Pays the Cable Bill Anyway?" *Political Affairs*, May 1996.
Charles McGrath	"The Internet's Arrested Development," *New York Times Magazine*, December 8, 1996.
Kathryn C. Montgomery	"Children in the Digital Age," *American Prospect*, July/August 1996. Available from PO Box 383080, Cambridge, MA 02238-3080.
Vincent Mosco	"Myths Along the Information Highway," *Peace Review*, March 1996.
Kim Nauer	"Holes in the Net," *City Limits*, March 1996.
PC World	"Electronic Commerce," October 1995.
Thomas E. Ricks	"Information-Warfare Defense Is Urged," *Wall Street Journal*, January 6, 1997.
Phillip E. Ross	"Cops Versus Robbers in Cyberspace," *Forbes*, September 9, 1996.
Louis Rossetto	"Cyberspace vs. the State," *Cato Policy Report*, May/June 1996.
Nathaniel Sheppard Jr.	"Without Access, It's a Road to Nowhere," *Emerge*, October 1996. Available from PO Box 7127, Red Oak, IA 51591-2127.
Julian Stallabrass	"Empowering Technology," *New Left Review*, May/June 1995.
Gene Stephens	"Crime in Cyberspace," *Futurist*, September/October 1995.
Jeff Ubois	"Eye on the Storm," *Internet World*, January 1997. Available from Mecklermedia, 20 Ketchum St., Westport, CT 06880.
Wall Street Journal	Special section on frequently asked questions about the Internet, December 9, 1996.
Stephen H. Wildstrom	"Ladies and Gentlemen: The Entertainer," *Business Week*, November 4, 1996.

Index